Praise for *Sparks in the Dark*

"Two fresh voices make a powerful case for providing students choice and authentic tasks as we guide them to become joyful and capable readers and writers. Travis and Todd speak from experience backed by research about what really works and does not work for students. Multiple examples from their own practice give readers a bird's-eye view of how literacy-rich schools and classrooms look. This book will surely spark productive conversations between teachers and teacher leaders. I can't wait to use *Sparks in the Dark* as a valuable tool in my consulting work!"

—Martha Page,
educational consultant, Adolescent Literacy & Learning, Inc.

"*Sparks in the Dark* is the rallying cry that Travis Crowder and Todd Nesloney hoped it would be! Their stories will inspire teachers to bring choice to the workshop so every student can find books that call them to the reading life and develop a lifelong passion for reading. You'll stand beside Travis as he helps students find their stories and write from their hearts. We learn through story, and Travis and Todd share stories about themselves, students, colleagues, and family that inspire creative thinking and guide and mentor us as we reflect on myriad teaching and leadership suggestions. Like a joyful refrain, stamped on every page is the importance of relationships and kindness to students. Truth be told, I couldn't put this book down, because as the authors note, their stories are 'glimpses of our hearts' that deeply touched my heart and sent me directly to stories about my students."

—Laura Robb,
teacher, coach, and author of *The Reading Intervention Toolkit*

"I said it twenty-five years ago and still believe it today: I am not the same teacher I was then, nor will I be the same teacher next year that I was this year. That is the way it should be. We are continually evolving as teachers and as learners. That is what Travis and Todd are showing us in this book—our students' growth is dependent on their teachers' growth. They are both passionate educators who are continually rethinking and changing their teaching practices based on what they know about their students and themselves as readers, writers, and learners. This is where they are right now—learners taking risks to be all they can be for the students in front of them at the moment. They offer us so many ways to be sparks in the dark as we grow as learners along with our students."

—Linda Rief,
8th-grade language arts teacher, Oyster River Middle School, Durham, NH
and author of *The Quickwrite Handbook, Read Write Teach*,
and *Inside the Writers'-Readers' Notebook*

"Come chase ideas with Travis and Todd as they disrupt the universe of reading and writing instruction. Ask students to join you on an endeavor of passion and joy and making meaning. Find the spark!"

—Jeff Anderson,
author of *Patterns of Power* and the Zack Delacruz series

"Travis and Todd open *Sparks in the Dark* with their shared commitment to create a rally cry that will inspire, challenge, and spark change. They bring this desire to life across the pages of this remarkable new book, illuminating the way to view reading and writing as a meaningful, purposeful, and yes, joyful experience. They celebrate books as the beating heart of our practices and weave in snapshots of what this could look like and sound like in classrooms and schools everywhere. I have no doubt that their words of wisdom will initiate rich collective conversations that will inspire us on a path toward disrupting our own educational universe in the name of kids."

—Mary Howard,
literacy consultant, author of *Good to Great Teaching*

"The authors' passion for enriching the reading and writing lives of children shines through in every word of *Sparks in the Dark*. They offer concrete activities for working with students and show the impact of their methods with real examples from the classroom. I developed a love of books as a child from the freedom I had to read whatever I wanted. As a homeschooling mom, I've never had to teach my children according to standards, tests, or reading levels and have attempted to instill a love of storytelling in them by letting them read and write freely according to their interests. Even so, *Sparks in the Dark* has opened my eyes further to new ways I can ignite my children's passion for stories and spark their interest in more diverse books. I found myself taking notes about how to improve the reading environment in my own home, show my children I value their own unique voices and identities, and become intentional in the books I choose to share with others. Highly recommended for educators, parents, and anyone who recognizes there is always room to learn, evolve, and grow as readers and writers."

—Dusti Bowling,
author of *Indescribable Events in the Life of a Cactus*

"*Sparks in the Dark* is a high-energy drink for teachers. Travis Crowder and Todd Nesloney invite readers to rethink (and yes, discard) hidebound traditions and to open classrooms to choice, passion, and authenticity. But what stands out for me is their sheer optimism and their willingness to experiment, take risks, and change.

"They are models and mentors who walk the walk. This book is a jolt we all need."

—Thomas Newkirk,
founder of The New Hampshire Literacy Institutes
and author of *(embarrassment): And the Emotional Underlife of Learning*

"With a stack of mentor authors holding them up, Travis and Todd are able to bring their professional and personal reading lives to their schools and now to the world. Through honest accounts and classroom application, this book sends the message that educators can always shift their practice to better the lives of their students. Travis and Todd have crafted a beautiful (and practical) narrative of their teaching lives."

—Sara K. Ahmed,
author, speaker, and literacy coach at
NIST International School, Bangkok, Thailand

"Travis Crowder and Todd Nesloney have crafted a book worthy of study by faculty groups across the country. In simple, straightforward language, they relate how they both came to embrace the reading/writing workshop approach, an approach that invites students to join the 'literacy club.' In addition to providing an overview of the approach, they break the reading/writing workshop down into its important components and suggest how teachers, librarians, and administrators might do so in their own schools. Plenty of personal stories about their journeys in literacy should make all readers feel as if they can make transitions to workshop approaches in classrooms. *Sparks in the Dark*, indeed."

—Teri Lesesne,
professor of library science at Sam Houston University in Houston, TX
and author of *Reading Ladders, Naked Reading,* and *Making the Match*

"Travis and Todd speak to the power of fine-tuning our practice and craft as educators through reading professional literature and active engagement in the professional community. Travis speaks to us in the voice of a classroom teacher striving to make instruction both authentic and deeply meaningful for his middle school students. Todd's voice opens a window into the thinking of a school administrator deeply involved in instructional leadership. Together they speak to the powerful influence of reading broadly and deeply, being involved in professional organizations such as NCTE and ILA and to being an active part of a larger professional community. Each section ends with an opportunity to pause and reflect, with a nudge to share your thinking with colleagues in a tweet. *Sparks in the Dark* is filled with energy and hope for a brighter future for our students and ourselves."

—Lester Laminack,
author and literacy consultant

"When I first read *Sparks in the Dark*, I thought Chapter 5, a chapter about giving kids choice in what they read, would be my favorite chapter. But then I read Chapter 6, a chapter about putting choice into the content areas, and that became my favorite chapter. Later, I was quite sure my favorite chapter was Chapter 9, which took up the topic of writing, and that held all the way through Chapter 10, which tackles revision. When I finished the book and started to put it on my bookshelf, I left it instead on my desk. Some books are like that: They need to be close because you'll turn to them often. They'll become dog-eared and coffee stained and filled with your notes as you make this book your own. *Sparks in the Dark* won't stay long on your bookshelf, but it will linger in your hands and will last longer in your thoughts."

—Kylene Beers,
coauthor of *Notice and Note, Reading Nonfiction,* and *Disrupting Thinking*

SPARKS in the DARK

Lessons, Ideas, and Strategies to *Illuminate* the Reading and Writing Lives in All of Us

Travis Crowder and Todd Nesloney

Published by Dave Burgess Consulting, Inc.
San Diego, CA
http://daveburgessconsulting.com

Cover Design by Genesis Kohler
Editing and Interior Design by My Writers' Connection

Library of Congress Control Number: 2018944108
Paperback ISBN: 978-1-946444-73-8
ebook ISBN: 978-1-946444-74-5

First Printing: May 2018

Dedication

To those who have inspired us
in our work with children.

To the sparks in the dark who are
lighting the way for all of us.
It's never easy, but you're not alone.
We each have a spark within us.

In memory of Sally Rost,
who lit a spark in many.

Contents

Foreword

L AST NIGHT I WALKED my dogs under a dark sky lit up by lamps. The stars spread across the sky behind our house and pierced the dark directly overhead. My dogs charged the snowbanks and barked at trees, while I leaned back to breathe in one of the gifts of living in the mountains of New Hampshire—endless stars.

Teachers need the blinking brilliance of tiny lights. We shrink next to mandates that dictate practices we know are not right for our students. We chafe against staff meetings that discourage us with trivia instead of helping us meet instructional challenges we face each day. We need colleagues lit with passion so we can rise beside their wise thinking. Passion is greater than standards and strategies. It is why we gather at conferences and read obsessively when we find an author who is a like-minded friend. In this book, you will find two: Todd Nesloney and Travis Crowder.

Todd and Travis are thoughtful, engaged professionals. You've probably read their posts on Twitter. Perhaps you watched Todd's TEDx talk. No doubt you've landed on Travis's blog posts that detail his quest to reach all readers. You will meet them anew in this book. They lead us into a conversation that has existed as long as there have been teachers fighting the loneliness of the classroom: We are stronger together.

This book glimmers with good ideas. Todd is a principal with heart. He tells the story of a staff meeting he filled with picture books. He asked teachers to partner across grade levels and brainstorm ways to use one of the books. This alone is smart work, but he takes it farther. He asks teachers to look at which books they chose and why. It creates a flash of understanding, a moment that resonates and challenges, and will no doubt live on in the thinking of his teachers. This is leadership that improves instruction.

There is a spark of playfulness here as well. Travis created mystery poems that he left on a shared document for students. He ignites an interest in language, in poetry, and in the joy of playing with images and ideas with his own poems. But he is also a model of vulnerability, living as a writer with his students. In *Sparks in the Dark* Travis shares his transformation into a teacher who writes and reminds us of the importance of practicing what we teach.

Todd and Travis do not shrink from hard conversations. They say, "When our reading lives are shallow, so is our teaching. It isn't an insult; it's the truth." They offer rich reading lists that have contributed to their own professional growth. They show us the spark of serious intellectual work. They remind us to stay vibrant as teachers.

May the light of this book remind you of your power.

PENNY KITTLE
Teacher, Author, Spark-Seeker
North Conway, New Hampshire
February 15, 2018

From a little spark
may burst a flame.
—Dante Alighieri

. . . a spark can set a
whole forest on fire.
just a spark.
save it.

—from Spark by
Charles Bukowski

Prologue

I N THE INTRODUCTION TO *Seeking Diversity*, author Linda Rief wrote, "I am not the same person who started teaching ten years ago. My classroom this year is very different from the way it was last year. I expect that—I want that. Several things have changed my thinking about what teaching and learning are all about."

Teaching is as much about teacher growth as it is about student growth. We encounter professional books, fiction books, colleagues, articles, and even students who challenge our way of thinking and nudge us further in our work as educators. Collectively, those influences help us develop our craft as teachers and influence our students and fellow teachers. Great teachers crave growth, and they seek challenges that will help them evolve as educators.

The two of us have been in education for a little more than a decade. During this time, we have read works from thinkers in our field who have shaped our practice, writers whose passion for teaching has changed the way we see our students and our role in their lives. As we peruse the beautiful writing of Thomas Newkirk, Penny Kittle, Nancie Atwell, Donalyn Miller, Linda Rief, Kylene Beers, Bob Probst, and a host of other authors, we know they are speaking from their current level of understanding. As they learn and grow and change, so does their writing. The same is true of us.

This book you hold in your hands represents the understanding we have come to at this point in our careers. We were graced with sparks that illuminated our darkness. A decade from now, our ideas will have changed, and our approaches will have evolved to meet the needs of our future students. Of one thing, we are certain. In the future, we will still need sparks to help chase away the darkness. We will need educators whose passion for teaching is formidable. We will need educators like you.

We want this book to guide your thinking and push you further in your teaching life. We want you to embrace the challenges that will change your practice and acquire the skills that will help you become a different, more determined, and effective teacher. This type of teaching, though, will require you to read and write alongside your students regardless of the subject you teach. We promise that we are growing right beside you.

Our hope is that you will be inspired by the lessons, writers, and ideas that have inspired us. We hope this book will be the spark that sets your passion for teaching on fire and renews your love for this great work we all do.

Rage, rage against the
dying of the light.

—Dylan Thomas

Chapter 1

The Literacy Imperative

EDUCATION HAS SEEN MORE major changes in the past decade than any single teacher can possibly synthesize. Standards, acronyms, policies, paperwork, and evaluations dominate our educational landscape. At the same time, students come into our classrooms, into a world filled with tight expectations, and they are, honestly, eager to learn. Their minds are full of questions, and they are curious about their world. They love doing science experiments, choosing their own books, reading those books aloud, and collaborating on projects. We know because we ask the students in our classes and in the schools we visit. What we find most often are students who abhor anything that interrupts the flow of learning. They do not describe their mindset in those exact terms, but their comments certainly convey that attitude. We hope *Sparks in the Dark* will create a rally cry, inspiring, challenging, and sparking changes, ones that will help other educators see how necessary meaningful reading and writing experiences are for students and teachers.

Meaningful teaching has always been necessary, but trends, programs, and fear often overtake education and pull us away from doing what we know is best for kids. We end up trying to find a silver bullet—that one research-based practice or district-mandated initiative that will help our students thrive like never before. Time and time again, we fall for the sales pitches and the beautifully designed data. We fall for the lie that a really good program is all it takes to change a child's educational trajectory. We focus all our attention on increasing a reading level, a test score, or the number of books read. We give in to our fear of failure and our fear of trying something new, and we cling to tired, ineffective tools such as worksheets and multiple-choice answers. It's safer that way, and for some of us, the reality is, if our kids don't perform the way our administration expects, our jobs might be on the line.

How can we change that?

The answer is simple, but its implications are huge. If our goal is to build our students' capacity as readers and writers, it is imperative that we participate in the process of reading and writing as well, in everything we do, in every subject we teach. It takes some work, yes, but the rewards of a rich reading and writing life are tremendous, and students will reap the benefits.

There is an alluring quality to every content area. The poetry of math, the metaphor of science, the humanity of history, and the literature of language arts combine to create a beautiful experience, all united by literacy. It is when these content areas are combined that they are potent and magical, and students can share the breathtaking view of the world that we, as educators, are privy to. Unfortunately, many of our students see school as a series of compartments, each with a skill set they must master before moving to the next grade. They do not have a chance to view the world through the lens of each subject area or see the threads that unite them.

Both of us come from a family of educators. It seems to run in our blood. We have experience at the high school, middle, and elementary levels as well as experience in school administration. Like so many professionals these days, we first met online through posts shared on our blogs and respective social media accounts. What started as a learning opportunity led to mutual respect and eventually a true friendship. Because of that friendship, we have enjoyed many open and honest conversations like the ones we hope to prompt with *Sparks in the Dark*. Conversations about instruction, classroom practices, beliefs about reading and writing, and so much more.

> If our goal is to build our students' capacity as readers and writers, it is imperative that we participate in the process of reading and writing as well, in everything we do, in every subject we teach.

In the past several years I (Todd) have gained a newfound passion for reading instruction and practices. My entire teaching career was in elementary school mathematics instruction. I loved it. I knew in high school I wanted to be a math teacher because I had always struggled with math as a student myself. I wanted to use the strategies I had learned to help other kids conquer their fears of math. In the classroom, I was that stereotypical math teacher. All about the numbers. We learned addition, subtraction, division, multiplication. We didn't read about math, and for several years, we didn't write about math. After all, my job was to teach math skills. Reading skills? That was the responsibility of my partner teacher across the hall. Boy, was I wrong.

During my first year as a principal, I read Donalyn Miller's *The Book Whisperer*, a professional book that speaks to the power of independent reading, of choice, and the joy that is created when students are given opportunities to read books that match their interests. I finished it while sitting on an airplane and was moved to tears. As I read the final words on the last page and closed the book my first thought was, "I want to go back into the classroom and teach reading!" You see, as a student I was an avid reader. In the fifth grade, I came across the *Animorphs* book series by K.A. Applegate and was hooked. I devoured books constantly, but I never incorporated that love of reading into teaching. It never even occurred to me. After reading Miller's book, my whole attitude toward reading and reading instruction shifted. I went back to my campus, bought her book for every staff member, and we began to read it and dive into our preconceived notions about reading and worked together on how we could promote that love of reading across our entire campus. I wrote about building that love of reading into our students in my book, *Kids Deserve It.*

As my team and I discussed this idea further, I read more books about reading and writing instruction and started connecting with other educators in this field through social media. I also diversified my own reading life, exploring fiction I had never previously considered. I saw my life changed when I read books such as *The Hate U Give* by Angie Thomas, *Serpent King* by Jeff Zentner, and *I'm Not Your Perfect Mexican Daughter* by Erika L. Sánchez. I watched my horizons expand, my mindsets shift, and my empathy deepen when I began to read about characters who looked and sounded nothing like me. Characters whose life experiences did not reflect my own. I connected with characters who dealt with racial profiling, death, loss, unique family dynamics, and prejudice. It gave me a new perspective about my students' experiences helping me see more clearly what they were going through in their daily lives. These books gave me a lens into my students' lives, a perspective that I had not previously possessed.

This kind of mindful reading changed everything for me. For the first time in my career, I truly understood the power that lies in stories. I began to see myself as more than just a math teacher or principal. I realized my role as an educator—no matter my subject specialty—is to use the tools of reading and writing to develop all of my students and staff. That insight has led to an awakening, a spark being lit that is impossible to extinguish. It's why I wanted to write this book with Travis and why I can't stop talking about this idea everywhere I go.

For Travis, it was a little different.

I (Travis) remember the moment the hard, honest truth hit me. It was a stinging, gut-wrenching truth I was resistant to accept. After seven years of teaching, after exploring complex themes in Shakespeare's *Hamlet* and *A Midsummer Night's Dream,* and guiding students through the desolation of Ray Bradbury's *Fahrenheit 451,* I had convinced myself I was doing the right thing. By choosing rigorous texts, I was sharpening my students' reading abilities, propelling them far beyond what any other educator had accomplished. Besides, if they could read the difficult stuff, testing would be easy.

My students demonstrated tremendous growth as a result of my instruction. Because my reading scores were improving, no administrator asked for my lesson plans or second-guessed my approach. I even talked up my students' reading gains when discussing my teaching methods with colleagues or attending district and state conferences. But deep down I knew the truth—none of my students were leaving my classroom with a love of reading and writing. Change was necessary.

I began sharing concerns with my coworkers, explaining that my students were largely resistant to my style of teaching. I had recently returned from the National Council of Teachers of English (NCTE) conference, and while there, I had gleaned a wealth of knowledge from writers and educators. The NCTE conference is a powerful experience and involves a supportive network of educators, of leaders in our field. I knew coming back that I wanted to read *The Book Whisperer* by Donalyn Miller and revisit *In the Middle* by Nancie Atwell. Atwell's book in particular was incredibly transformative early in my career. I remember reading it having my mind blown with the idea that students could actually be engaged in the act of reading and writing. When I paired what I learned from *In the Middle* with what Donalyn talks about in *The Book Whisperer,* I was provided with a tool chest full of ideas that would alter the way I viewed reading and writing instruction forever. I had experimented with nontraditional classroom teaching and the outcome had been subpar, but I was willing to try again.

Within a week, I had finished *The Book Whisperer*, and by the time I returned from spring break, I was ready to implement a reading and writing workshop as an initiative in my eighth-grade classes. In a workshop classroom, emphasis is placed on student interest and choice in their reading and writing lives. It is less focused on lecture and more on the application and acquisition of skills.

My students were not sure what to think about the markedly different curriculum I was offering, especially when they fell in love with books and could not stop talking about their reading lives.

In retrospect, I am filled with gratitude when I consider this moment in my teaching life. Since then, my professional library has grown exponentially, and my Twitter feed is filled with updates from professionals I respect and adore. Their thinking and leadership improve my teaching and the education my students receive. Most importantly, I have come to understand that books matter, reading matters, and without either, students' educational experiences suffer.

> When you teach someone how to read
> or how to express themselves using the
> written word, you change a life.

We believe this book matters because reading and writing are the foundation of all we do. When you teach someone how to read or how to express themselves using the written word, you change a life. You introduce them to magical worlds, teach them how to access the voice within, and empower them to affect that same change in the lives of others. You also learn to take resistance seriously, understanding that pushback from students might be a sign that coursework is too difficult, possibly irrelevant, and might not have been as astounding as you thought.

Education is important. We all know that. Equally important is building a true love of reading and writing. That inexorable need to escape into a world far different from your own. That drive to learn more about people who changed the course of history or unravel a mystery. The experience of feeling as if characters are truly family as you walk through their struggles with them. Or the moment the words you struggled to say aloud finally flow from your pen onto the page.

Those are the sparks in the dark we want our students to have because, in those moments, lives are truly changed.

THINGS TO THINK ABOUT AND TWEET

Why is reading and writing important to you?

How has a character in a book
affected you personally?

How do you view reading or writing in your
own life? Do you enjoy it? Approach it with
ambivalence? Fear it? And why?

#SparksInTheDark

Do I dare disturb
the universe?

—T.S. Eliot

Chapter 2

Disturbing the Universe

EVEN TODAY, IN 2018, the discipline of language arts is often taught in a traditional manner. Almost every school has at least one classroom where students are all reading the same novel, at the same pace, and completing the same activities. Writing prompts are teacher-generated, and student responses often lack voice and passion. In some classrooms, reading passages are handed out weekly, and students are asked to closely read the text and answer multiple-choice questions, an assignment designed to simulate test-taking. Although administered with the best of intentions, these practices are destructive and can cause students to loathe reading. We're here to tell you those are not your only choices. In fact, we believe it's possible to instill in your students a love of reading and writing and help them pass a standardized exam.

The current trend is to require students to follow the same reading pace, complete worksheets for arbitrary grades, and respond to questions that do not inspire creative and critical thinking. Completing a worksheet or a graphic organizer just to fulfill an assignment does not equate to learning. It only equates to compliance. Part of our goal with this book is to contribute to that ongoing conversation about teaching practices. We want to curb this current trend of traditional teaching that has students going through works of literature at a collective pace, and assignments are not differentiated to meet the needs of all students. This will require major change.

Change, in all of its intricate forms, is difficult. It pushes us outside of our comfort zones. But change isn't meant to be easy. If it were, everyone would love and seek out change.

> Change isn't meant to be easy.
> If it were, everyone would
> love and seek out change.

When we have an established curriculum, solid routines, written lesson plans and effective activities that we enjoy, it's easy to submerge our creativity beneath waves of complacency. But when we are committed to our students' learning and want to see them grow as readers, writers, and thinkers, we will choose to take a closer look at the expectations we hold for our students and the work we assign. We will view reading and writing as skills that should be valued beyond language arts and incorporated into all content areas including math, science, and social studies.

In my (Travis) teaching life, abandoning a traditional form of teaching and adopting a reading and writing workshop approach has been my way of disturbing the universe. Reading and writing workshops are based on choice. Students choose their books. Focus is on skill acquisition. Teachers do not lecture; instead, mini-lessons are used, and students are given time to practice the skills taught during the mini-lesson. In writing workshop, writers choose their topics, chasing ideas through poetry, essay, memoir, or short story. The teacher teaches the features of different genres and gives students time to craft and share their writing. There are naysayers, those who look down their noses at such an approach, but I have seen the delight in students' eyes, their growth as readers, and their willingness to write because of the reading and writing workshop.

They have developed an interest in reading, a passion for writing, and a commitment to the learning process. And they trust me more. In social studies, I incorporate poems, articles, book chapters, images, letters, and infographics to initiate small- and large-group conversations, writing, and further reading. I weave conversations about books into specific lessons. "There's a book about this topic," I say to my students, taking the time to grab the book off the shelf and read a few excerpts to pique their interest. Not all of them will read the book, but some do.

Book talks are perfect as a jumping-off point when introducing a social studies or language arts lesson. The choices are endless. You can explore nonfiction history, biographies, or contemporary novels to enhance a specific unit of study. For instance, right now in one of my seventh-grade classes, we are discussing exploration—why people seek answers to questions that plague them, even when there is a risk involved. I used the poem "Mercy, after Nikki Giovanni" and the book *Newfoundland* by Allan Wolf to nudge students' thinking about exploration and the moral obligations of those who explore.

Although book talks and reading aloud might seem more naturally suited to an elementary classroom, they are also great tools for secondary classrooms. The kids are older, and that means they can see through you in a second, but sometimes it pays off to speak from the heart, be honest, maybe even a little vulnerable, and share your love of a specific book. When students see your genuine passion and interest, it will pique theirs.

Meaningful Learning

Like many educators, our teaching lives have been in a constant state of evolution. Once upon a time, we were those teachers who created packets and worksheets for students to complete during a class period.

Why, you may ask? Easy answer. Worksheets and packets are simple for the instructor. Students fill in the blanks, cite their evidence, hand in the worksheet or packet, and receive a grade. Sometimes we even found ourselves labeling our worksheets as "Close Reading Assignments" or "Math Fun," thinking that nomenclature would affect students' perception of the work. But it did not. And honestly, it never does.

No worksheet or packet will ever supersede the passion a teacher can ignite. We have never witnessed students who are joyous about a content area when their experiences are limited to fill-in-the-blank answers. We understand these practices might be deemed necessary in some situations, but when they make up the majority of class instruction, students are the ones to suffer. Meaningful learning experiences are critical if we want students to learn because these experiences compel their hearts, ignite their curiosity, and engage their minds in reading and writing.

> No worksheet or packet
> will ever supersede the
> passion a teacher can ignite.

Throughout this book, we have included multiple questions, activities, and ideas to inspire more creative thinking in your teaching life. There is a beautiful benefit from watching students grapple with a question, an idea, or an alternative view they had not considered. Renouncing worksheets and packets gives you breathing room as an educator and allows students to do their own thinking. We know because we have seen both sides of this issue, in our own classrooms and in the classrooms of colleagues.

Meaningful Teaching

We love *In the Middle* by Nancie Atwell, and when talking with teachers about best practices and ideas that will transform a classroom, we always return to her seminal text. In one part of the book, Atwell describes her belief in a reading and writing workshop, a style of teaching that does not follow a program and is not weighed down by irrelevant assignments and projects. Even at the top of a lesson plan book, she scratches out the "English/Language Arts" heading and writes "Writing and Reading Workshop." There is tremendous value in Nancie Atwell's thinking. We prefer to view our classes as workshops, as places where students work with skills and ideas, seeking to interact with the world through writing and problem-solving. Meaningful teaching gives students space to grapple with issues, such as social and economic concerns, and to explore the world around them through books and conversation. From this type of thinking and teaching emerges complexity and depth, which are necessary components of meaningful, intentional teaching.

Students know when their teachers mean what they teach. They can sense your convictions about a subject area. Teaching is most meaningful when we live it. Anyone who walks in our classroom or office will notice our libraries, large bookshelves that are still growing. They will see a whiteboard ledge with books that showcase a current reading life, as well as ones that we feel will be impactful in their lives that they may not otherwise gravitate towards. They can see a sign outside our classrooms and offices that advertises what we might be currently reading. They will also see walls covered in evidence of our learning and learning processes.

Meaningful teaching doesn't just happen in front of our students. As a principal now, I (Todd) see how important it is for me to share information with my team with the same enthusiasm I once used in my fifth-grade classroom. If you think kids can see right through your forced and faked passion, adults are even better at it!

Every month I have a faculty meeting. I've seen the memes online about how painful faculty meetings can be, and I get it. I've endured a few that made me want to poke out my eyes. I try really hard to make our faculty meetings a time of connecting with each other and learning something new.

We often start our meetings with a crazy game or a funny or moving YouTube video (SoulPancake has some great choices!). Then we move into a preplanned learning activity. One of my favorites was when I laid out more than fifty picture books on a table. I have quite the collection in my office as I love finding books to read with classrooms. I choose books with a wide variety of characters, authors, illustrators, and stories about everything from incarcerated parents to children with disabilities to talking animals who teach a lesson to children growing up in other countries.

I asked each staff member to partner up with someone from a different grade level. Their task was to select a book together—one that spoke to both of them—by looking only at the cover, read it together and discuss how to use the story within their classrooms. Across the room, the different pairs of teachers bonded over their stories. It was amazing to hear a fifth-grade teacher sharing with a kindergarten teacher, brainstorming different ways they could each use the same story.

After they had some time to read and talk, I asked each pair to find another pair of teachers and pitch their book to generate interest. It was a powerful activity and one I plan to use in future meetings.

Afterward, I asked a few volunteers to stand and share the ideas that were discussed and then asked five people to pitch their book before the whole group. It went wonderfully!

What my team didn't realize, though, is I was setting them up. I always have something else up my sleeve—and it keeps them on their toes! What my staff, who is predominately white though our students are not, didn't realize is out of the fifty books I placed on the tables, ten had lead characters who were minorities or children with disabilities.

> We must be diligent
> in choosing books that
> don't just reflect
> our views and upbringing.

Out of the twenty-four books that were selected by my teacher teams, only two were the more diverse books. I used this moment to talk to my team about that natural tendency to gravitate towards stories that reflect your own life. Characters who look like us, sound like us, and live like we do. We don't always do it intentionally, but until we realize we're doing it, we don't change it. I wanted our teacher teams to see we must be intentional when selecting books for our classrooms. We must be diligent in choosing books that don't just reflect our views and upbringing. It was an eye-opening moment and one I hope will have repercussions throughout our building as we continue to diversify our libraries.

When We Disturb

When we disturb the universe, we sometimes find ourselves standing alone, charging into battle with no one on our side, or so it seems. Upsetting the applecart can cause others to step back. How many times have you heard a colleague say, "I'm not doing that project. It's way too much work!" or "Can you stop doing those kinds of things? If admin sees, they'll want all of us to do that nonsense." Yes, disturbing the universe can, at times, be lonely, but we've both found the rewards are well worth a little isolation.

We've also found social media to be the place where we are able to find others who will disturb alongside us. We are always careful, however, not to create an echo chamber—a cozy little nook where everyone agrees with you and no one questions you. We seek out those who will challenge our thinking, accept no excuses, and always encourage us to do what's best for kids.

We have seen the power social media has to connect us to professional networks beyond our individual campuses. It has allowed us to find other educators who help us develop our ideas and extend our thinking, which are critical actions in a teaching life. These educators have inspired us to move forward, especially when fear of failure and uncertainty had momentarily immobilized us.

We know it is easy to do things the way we have always done them, using the strategies and teaching tools used on us when we were students. We settle for the comfortable and the tried-and-true. But we don't have to! We can change our approach, step outside the norm, and move our students to deeper thinking, deeper writing, and deeper learning. We can give them a reason to fall in love with education, reigniting the curiosity and passion they had for school and learning earlier in their lives.

We can push through the uncomfortable, the painful, the failures, and charge ahead, even if we have to step out alone. It's up to us to disrupt the universe, and we want you to join us.

THINGS TO THINK ABOUT AND TWEET

In what ways are you
disturbing the universe?

How have you faced pushback to new ideas,
and what have you done to forge ahead?

What is something you're ready
to go back and try again?

#SparksInTheDark

Dreams lurk in books. We must never forget that. We have been given the privilege of this life in teaching. Let us have the strength to start where they are and lead them.

—Penny Kittle

Chapter 3

It Starts with a Bookshelf

A **BOOKSHELF IS ONE OF** those things that's far more than the sum of its parts. Its wood and metal and hardware combine to form a kind of portal into other worlds. The books it holds offer stories that can entertain for hours on end, leaving us laughing uncontrollably or sobbing in tears. A simple bookshelf in the corner of a classroom contains more magic and excitement than we can possibly imagine.

We delight in watching our students connect with a book that moves them and invites them on a journey of mystery, adventure, suspense, or discovery. We love how they seek out a quiet, comfortable place in the classroom and begin to read, captivated by every word. Their imaginations dance with curiosity as they work to understand the characters they encounter and travel with them to find answers, to vanquish foes, or to reunite with lost or forgotten friends. They enter the realm of the story and forget about the world around them, cognizant only of the issues within the context of the book.

Books have the ability to transport us. They help us deal with our pain and gain empathy for others. They help us dream big dreams and travel to places that exist only in our imagination. They provide a place of comfort and solace. They can be our friends when we are isolated. Books are powerful. They're transformative and life-altering. But what about our students who don't have access to books, and do not see a variety of options in front of them?

Many schools have libraries. Some of these schools are even so lucky as to have a certified librarian running that library! School libraries provide wonderful opportunities for children to find and treasure the perfect book. But when a library is the only place in a school where students can find a variety of books, that's a problem. Why should the library be the sole source of books in a school?

Schools across the country have become filled with children who have had their passion for reading replaced with packets, worksheets, and test preparation. A child's love of reading quickly diminishes under the weight of a curriculum focused on answering multiple-choice questions or getting the right answer. So where do we even begin? How do we battle something so ingrained in our school environments?

The first step is making a choice. As educators we have to reflect and determine if we believe our packets and test prep are more important than a joyful reading experience. When we come to the obvious conclusion that our job is to nurture and cultivate that love of reading, we know we need to change. But sometimes because of the weight of the curriculum, the district mandates, and the countless other burdens that are put upon us, we struggle to decide how we can change when there is a conflict of interest.

But change can take place. Whether it's as simple as starting an after-school book club with a few of your students (or fellow teachers), building a Little Free Library, advertising what you are reading outside your door, or even just sharing the book you are currently reading with your students, change can happen. It is in your hands.

What about the Adult Readers We've Lost?

Not every adult has a robust reading life or an experience with books that has endeared them to the act of reading. Unfortunately, many adults do not view themselves as readers. So how are they going to fill a room with books or get kids excited about reading? It starts with finding books you love and building a reading life sustained by interest and choice and grounded by a passion and love for reading.

A startling statistic, published by the Pew Research Center in November 2016, revealed that twenty-six percent of American adults had not read an entire book in the previous year. As a voracious reader and English teacher, this percentage frightens me because it represents a significant portion of our nation's adults. These statistics are sobering, especially when we take into account our role as educators.

In *Minds Made for Stories*, Thomas Newkirk writes brilliantly about our need for narrative and characters and the need to see them come to a resolution. He also explores our need for a sense of plot as we look at numbers, synthesizing data and seeking to understand it. If there is a narrative to the numbers, meaning behind them, possibly a conflict that caused a shift in the numbers, our awareness of the data's significance increases. We are primed for stories, Newkirk argues. And he is right.

Newkirk's argument throughout *Minds Made for Stories*, a compelling read for any educator, helped us make better sense of the results from the Pew Research Center. Even though a story was not presented to us, we began looking for one. Implied in these statistics is the role of the teacher. Educators have power, much more than we may realize. We can enforce a whole-class reading regimen, limiting the reading lives of students to the books we select or we can allow students to select their own books, guiding them to develop their own reading identities.

Each day we interact with adults whose reading lives are paltry. They are quick to admit they do not read, and sometimes we hear them tell students too. Appalled as we are, we try to remember the narrative within the Pew Research Center results. Adults who do not read were usually children who did not read. As educators, it is imperative we make every concerted effort to help students build a reading life in our classes while we have them. If we want students to read compelling literature in all subject areas, we have to give them a starting point. More than anything, we want them to grow into adults who read. We have the power to make that happen. We are responsible for them.

> ## Adults who do not read were usually children who did not read.

We have talked to countless teachers who say they teach math or science because they never really cared for reading. Heck, we've even come across reading teachers who don't read anything in their own personal lives.

How can this be? Where did it go wrong? We are sure some of you reading this book now might only be reading it because your school or administrator assigned it as something to be read and discussed as a staff. No one loves every book they pick up. And for struggling readers, even as adults, if they don't connect with the characters or content, they aren't going to read it. If all they have ever been fed is one disconnected book after another, they stop reading. Many people view themselves as nonreaders, but we challenge that notion. We believe you simply haven't found the right book yet.

Another obstacle is time. We are all busy; we get that. But these days reading can take many time-saving forms. Sometimes it's picking up a comic book filled with rich characters or listening to a new selection on audiobook during a jog or drive, or flipping through your favorite magazine in the grocery store line. Readers read. They devour everything around them. And the more they read, the more natural it becomes, and the more they find themselves making time for it.

We don't allow our students to make excuses in school for why they don't feel like learning a new math problem, science experiment, or writing strategy. So why do we allow ourselves to make excuses for why we aren't growing from the books we're reading or not reading?

We Are Responsible for All Readers

When I (Travis) began teaching, I believed I was obligated to expose my students to as much classic literature as possible. Convinced that reading these texts was the only way to ensure my students studied and analyzed rigorous literature, we delved into William Shakespeare, Edgar Allan Poe, Emily Dickinson, Walt Whitman, Langston Hughes, and Maya Angelou. We generated thoughts and ideas about how each of these writers viewed the world and how those ideas could still inspire the current generation. In all honesty, I should rephrase that. I generated the thoughts and ideas, and my students went along with them. At the end of the year, their ideas about reading had not changed. Although I had exposed them to all sorts of great literature, none of my students had developed a burning desire to read. None of my students had established a reading life.

I believe the classics play an important role in language arts because this kind of literature forms the foundation for language and thematic study. The beautiful language of *Hamlet* gives students a lens through which to view politics and humanity. Landscape and poetry frame the narrative of Emily Brontë's *Wuthering Heights*, allowing readers to explore the wildness of the moors and the turmoil of romance. I love the books, plays, and poems in this canon, and respect their placement. Not all literature worth reading, though, is housed within its conceptual walls.

Quality reading instruction does not begin with literature. It begins with students. English classes can be magical places, but they have the potential to become sources of anxiety and boredom, places where journeys of the mind are hindered by scavenger hunts for literary devices or quizzes that impose compliance. We believe that we are responsible for all readers in our classrooms, and if students are not reading the books we are assigning, we must make changes. Common texts are important, and there is merit to having a whole-class conversation about one story or book. In such an environment, students have the chance to hear other perspectives, challenge their own thinking, and argue their opinions—skills needed for all content areas. There is, however, great value and necessity in the development of an independent reading life, and without it, students will merely comply or pretend to comply with arbitrary reading expectations. They won't experience the transformative love of reading that can sustain them well beyond the classroom and into adulthood.

Like many educators, we meet students who have already developed a sense of book love, those who are constantly sharing book recommendations with us and others and sneaking popular reads out of our classroom libraries. Quite a few of these voracious readers have read classics such as *To Kill a Mockingbird*, *Fahrenheit 451*, and *Hatchet*. Their willingness to read these works encourages us in our work, but we truly earn our stripes when we can lead our students to books that will capture their individual interests. In fact, it's the first obstacle to clear in creating a reading life. When we take responsibility for every reader in our classrooms, we are pledging to help students build and sustain their personal and independent reading life.

At the beginning of each year, we have started giving our students a reading inventory, asking them to identify books they have read, favorite authors, and genres they find compelling. Nonreaders rarely have a favorite author or book, but if we can identify their interests, we can usually get them interested in a book. Many times, we have taken the time to create a preview stack, an idea we adopted from Donalyn Miller. We create a stack of five to ten books, telling students that they only have to pick one, but if none of the books suit their interests, we will try again. As an administrator or a classroom teacher, you can easily take the time to pitch a stack of books to any hungry reader. Taking a brief ownership of their book selection lets them know we are interested in them academically. We want to see them succeed, and we care about them. We've never had a student return a full stack to either of us.

In our classrooms, we also study common texts such as classic short stories, poems, articles, Shakespearean monologues, and book chapters. Our students will use these common texts to practice a variety of skills, including analyzing character and understanding symbolism. In general, we seek texts that align with student interests and are thematically related to popular books in the classroom library.

Taking responsibility for all readers means knowing their interests and searching for the books that will captivate them. Our students will never know the excitement of reading unless we show them how beautiful stories really are and help them build and sustain a reading life. Taking responsibility for all readers also means committing to creating an environment where students have time to read, discuss, write, and think about books. Within our classrooms, we must provide our students with the physical space necessary for comfortable reading—a place where books and all that they entail are the priority. We can't wait for others to show our students the value of books and reading, and we can't expect our students to figure it out on their own. We are the ones we've been waiting for!

> Taking responsibility for all readers
> means knowing their interests and searching
> for the books that will captivate them.

Bookshelves Outside the Language Arts Classroom

Students of all ages should see books and bookshelves and hear book talks all over their schools—not just in their language arts classrooms. One of the established norms we have seen throughout schools is the notion that classroom libraries are only for English classrooms. Reading is relegated to ELAR classrooms only, while other content areas, such as science and social studies, are book deserts. All content areas are rich with literacy, but when we fail to put libraries in all classrooms, we imply that books and reading are only necessary in English classes.

As a principal and former math teacher, I (Todd) have seen first-hand the importance of incorporating books into every aspect of a school. When we put bookshelves only in the library or in language arts classrooms, and we pitch books only in those locations, our students immediately compartmentalize their learning. They start to believe those are the only places reading needs to happen.

I have been adamant about making access to books a priority at my school, Webb Elementary. I started with my office. As the school principal, I deal with all kinds of students all day. Students who are in trouble, who need time to cool down, who are struggling, and who need to be celebrated for great choices. What I love most is connecting with them through a book or a story. I have two large bookshelves in my office. One is filled with picture books and the other is packed with chapter books and novels. I've made a conscious effort to ensure those shelves offer books filled with diverse characters with rich storylines.

From the moment visitors reach our front door, it's clear we take books seriously. Books are readily available from a Little Free Library we have in front of the school and in our office waiting area. In the corners of our hallways, we have bookshelves filled with books students can borrow and return as needed. I have found money in our campus budget to ensure we are providing every classroom library with books. Whether kindergarten or fifth-grade science, it is important for every classroom to grow its library with high-interest and diverse texts. This process has not been quick or easy, but when you are passionate about it, you can make it happen!

At Webb, we don't allow negative voices to slow our roll. Through organizations such as Donors Choose and Scholastic, we gather all the resources and research we can to support our mission to fill our school with books. Not only do we light the fire in our students, we help them spread it through unique opportunities such as the "Secret Society of Readers" and "Book Prom," which I write about at length in *Stories from Webb*.

Don't be intimidated! If you're a teacher who's passionate about reading and looking for ways to share that passion with your students and colleagues, it can be done. You could start an after-school book club for your fellow teachers or a few students, organize a family literacy night at your school, hold a "book tasting" and invite students to come by during lunch to browse and snack. Maybe you're on your own. Maybe you won't have anyone helping you. Do it anyway! Be a spark in the dark. In time it just might become a blaze that lights up your entire campus with a love of reading.

Next Steps

If we're modeling reading and working to help our students fall in love with books, our students must be able to access books in a variety of locations. Every classroom—even those subjects where reading usually isn't emphasized—should have a bookshelf filled with a variety of options for children to explore and investigate. Access to books in all classrooms is essential, and these books should contain myriad perspectives, important lessons about life, diverse characters, and ideas that will stretch students' thinking. Without a diverse, full library and unconditional access to it, students will never experience the joy that comes from reading.

> Without a diverse, full library and unconditional access to it, students will never experience the joy that comes from reading.

As a classroom teacher, it is your responsibility to motivate your students to read, and you can't do that if you yourself are not reading. And we're not just talking about the newest professional development books. We're talking graphic novels, young adult fiction, adult contemporary fiction, middle grades novels, adult and young adult nonfiction, comic books, magazines, audiobooks, and so on.

This applies to teachers in all content areas. Too often we relegate the role of building readers and writers to the English or language arts teachers. That kind of tunnel vision not only misses the point, but it also does our students a disservice. It teaches children to compartmentalize their learning, and they come to believe reading only happens when a reading teacher tells you to pick up a book for silent reading time or an assignment.

Language arts, math, science, social studies, and every subject in between should be creating a diverse library in their classrooms for kids to pull from at any moment. Imagine a school environment where a child never has to utter the words, "I don't have a book," because every space on campus has an easy-to-reach bookshelf. We must start seeing ourselves as educators who are working to build a love of reading within our students, regardless of our content area. What books about math, aside from technical, obtuse ones, would students read and love? What books about science, other than textbooks, will demonstrate to students how a story is powerful even in a non-English/language arts field? What novel would you pick up and begin reading with a social studies class to give them a narrative-based view of history? Reading and writing are the fundamental elements of all content areas, and if we're not all working together to reflect that reality, we'll never truly help our children reach their full potential and unlock the empathy and compassion that lies within each of them.

In this effort, administrators are equally responsible. We must help teachers gain access to books as well. Budgets are tight; we get it. But when there's a choice between ordering more workbooks or some new-fangled computer program, why not choose to put more books in teachers' hands? That might mean hosting book drives at your school or helping teachers fill out Donors Choose projects (an online crowd-funding website) or even buying every student a book using Scholastic bucks. The only real limitation placed on providing classrooms with more books is the limitation we place on ourselves by not thinking outside the box. It's easy for administrators to tell teachers to provide the books themselves, but we all know how wealthy all of us in the education world are. It's time for administrators to start reading more as well and advertising the books they are reading. It's time for administrators to find the funding or other resources to place countless, high-quality and high-interest books in the hands of their teachers and students. The idea that it takes a village truly does apply here.

What Do You Do When . . . ?

What do you do when your administrator will not purchase books for your classroom?

- Visit local bookstores or thrift stores, searching for bargain-priced books.

- Ask friends on social media if they have anything they would be willing to donate.

- Complete a Donors Choose project.

- Send a letter home to parents, asking them to send previously enjoyed books to your classroom.

What do you do when you don't know how to start selecting books for your classroom library?

- Identify the award-winning books from current or recent years. These would include, but are not limited to, the National Book Award, Pura Belpré Award, Stonewall Award, Newbery Award, and the Coretta Scott King Award.

- Visit WeNeedDiverseBooks.org for titles that are diverse and reflective of all types of students.

- Ask your students their interests. Use reading inventories to identify the types of stories your students will love.

- Post a "Books We Need in Our Classroom Library" wish list. Allow students—and even parents—to add books to this list. You might consider creating a digital version so students and parents can add to this list at their leisure.

What do you do when no one else around you is a reader?

- Try to generate interest by sending emails to your coworkers, inviting them to your classroom to discuss books.

- Find your tribe online. Begin posting about books you have read that have moved and inspired you.

- Join monthly book chats on Twitter.
- Join the conversation with the #SparksInTheDark hashtag.

In the end, it's so much more than just providing a bookshelf. We need to be doing book talks, sharing our favorites, and helping students find theirs. Classrooms are not the only places where bookshelves should be full and visible. Administrators should have bookshelves in their offices for kids to pull from. We should have bookshelves full of books in our front foyers, in our gyms and cafeterias, and in our hallways. And when we can take advantage of a Little Free Library, we should do it!

Reading changes lives. It gives people opportunities and experiences they can't get anywhere else. Until we start providing our students with a limitless supply of books, they might not find the one that gets them hooked and leads to a life of #BookLove.

It starts with a simple bookshelf: that location in a bedroom, classroom, office or library where children know they can go and find a book that will take them on a journey unlike any other.

THINGS TO THINK ABOUT AND TWEET

What are the obstacles you feel are standing in your way of building a diverse and rich classroom library?

What's the first thing you can do to bring that love of reading into your space or a new space at your school?

#SparksInTheDark

The point, I tell them and you, is to be in the game, to be at the table, to be a part of the conversation, to contribute what is yours to give, to help all those who come along behind you to not just be part of the story, but to be one who helps write that story.

—Jim Burke

Chapter 4

Professional Responsibility in Teaching

READING AND WRITING ARE the collective essence of education. Each content area we teach has literacy at its core, and within and around that core are people who have written and continue to write about it. Most educators' initial impression of teaching is very technical: A teacher disseminates information and students take notes; there are moments to write, moments to read, and there are plenty of tests and quizzes. There might even be bursts of creativity where students were asked to write from their hearts. As a writing teacher, the biggest letdown is when students walk to your desk, with written responses in their hands, proclaiming they are finished with the assignment after writing for only several minutes. And, of course, you think, "How can you be finished? How, in ten minutes, can you write, reread, revise, and edit your work?"

Sometimes you might hear students complaining and saying, "I don't know what to write." You're thinking, "How can you *not* think of a topic to write? You talk all the time. You've even lied to me on multiple occasions. Surely there's a story burgeoning within you." Yet, they are unable to find that story, and after several failed attempts at writing, we abandon hope in their writing ability.

Independent reading can feel much the same way. Students don't always know what they are interested in or what genres appeal to them, so, in defeat and compliance, they choose a random book from a shelf in the school library. Students who use this method to select books are rarely interested in them. They get the needed answers from these books to complete the assignment the teacher prescribes, and joylessly, they bring it to class each day to read.

When asked to write, students often produce shallow pieces that are only an exercise in compliance. Mostly, we ask students to respond to questions we pose, to ideas, to thinking that has inspired us. The writing they are producing is merely a regurgitation of class discussion. There might be occasions when we ask students to write creatively, to tell stories, write poems, and think deeply about a topic and write from their hearts. But it's never enough.

Teaching students to read and write from the heart is not easy, and it requires cultivation.

We wish we could say this kind of teaching happens only during a teacher's first year, but many of us used this approach for years before seeing the error of our ways. Teaching students to read and write from the heart is not easy, and it requires cultivation. A teacher must become a guide, a mentor, and an example, demonstrating clearly what it takes to read and write effectively. In this chapter, we will explore the teacher as reader and the teacher as writer, investigating ways to help our students hone reading and writing skills, develop individual interests, find their own voices, and appreciate the power of story.

The Teacher as Reader

At the end of my (Travis) first year of teaching, on the very last day, one of my homeroom students walked to my desk and confidently told me he would be traveling to the beach for part of the summer. Pleasantries were exchanged and feeling an end to his story, I moved behind my desk to begin packing up my things: books I had collected from the discard pile in the school library, a stack of articles, and mementos, a file folder of lesson ideas for the following year, and my broken watch (I still have it, by the way, and it is still broken). The young boy remained where he was, his posture and facial expression indicating the conversation was not yet over. So, I waited.

"What are your plans this summer?"

"I want to read!" I answered immediately and with a broad smile.

He stared at me, and I knew what was going through his mind. With all the things to do during the summer, why would I choose to read? Books were for school, not pleasure. And based on my teaching that year, I wasn't surprised. He did not say those words to me, but I could tell, based on his eye roll and chortle, that's what he was thinking. When the final bell of the year rang, my summer vacation began, and I read like a fiend. Honestly, I felt like I had been starved of books. I read *The Collector* and *The Magus* by John Fowles, *Love in the Time of Cholera* by Gabriel García Márquez, *The Shadow of the Wind* by Carlos Ruiz Zafón, *You Can't Go Home Again* by Thomas Wolfe, and *The Secret History* by Donna Tartt. I even ventured into the professional realm and read *From Hinton to Hamlet* by Sarah Herz and Donald Gallo. By the end of the summer, I was refreshed and entered the classroom for my second year, but when it ended, I needed the same reading recovery program from the summer before.

It never occurred to me that my personal reading life had a place in my classroom. My reading habits are driven by interest and passion, a need for research, and whimsy. I am a good reader because I read. And I read a lot. In Pernille Ripp's book, *Passionate Readers*, she discusses how she compartmentalized her teaching and reading lives, never converging the two until she realized taking her reading life into the classroom could benefit her students. I was much the same.

After attending the NCTE conference in Minneapolis a few years ago, I returned to my classroom with a renewed interest in reading and discussing books with students. I abandoned the traditional format of instruction I had grown accustomed to and established my room as a reading zone. Conferences became a norm during independent reading time, and students expected me to arrive at their desks with my clipboard, legal pad, pen, and often, a book recommendation. After necessary conferences, I took a seat somewhere in the classroom, often in my chair, and read along with them.

My library grew as my knowledge of young adult literature increased. As I recommended these young adult books to my students, their interest in reading soared, magnified by the time I gave them to preview and read these books in class. As they discovered books they loved, they developed allegiances to particular authors and genres. A poster by my door was a place for them to indicate books they wanted me to purchase for the classroom library, and over time, we created a wonderful collection of books. Within several months, my classes had read a combined total of 1,200 books, and it all started with a desire to share books and take my personal reading life into the classroom.

When teachers present themselves as readers, it becomes clear to their students that books are a priority, and their classrooms are a place where books are welcome and valued. If they want their students to perform well on tests that assess their ability to read, they must expect their students to read. They must demonstrate that reading isn't an activity that happens only in a classroom or to complete an assignment. Reading is part of a well-rounded life.

As a school principal, I (Todd) have seen what happens when reading truly takes over a campus. In fact, I made reading a focal point of my office when I decided to give it a makeover a few years ago. The first thing I did was get rid of my giant brown desk. You know the one I'm talking about—it's that desk you see in every movie or TV portrayal of a school principal. When it was gone, I was shocked at how much room I had, so I purchased a small rectangular table for parent conferences and other work. I wanted the rest of the office to be a kid-friendly space, so I filled it with some comfortable chairs, a nice rug, and quite a few art supplies and games. But the best part was my centerpiece—a giant bookshelf packed with all the books I had been collecting for the past few years.

I find it exciting to work with children who claim to hate reading because much of the time the problem is they simply haven't found a book that grips their heart or reaches their soul. And I know I can be that gateway to characters and stories that can ignite a lifelong love of reading.

I remember working with a young girl who would act out every day in her reading class. Her teacher had run out of patience and called me down to the room to speak with the student. After pulling the little girl out of class to chat, I asked her what was going on and why was she so upset. I asked her if she was tired, angry, or if the work was too hard. She told me, "Mr. Nesloney, none of those things are the problem. We are asked to read every day in class for at least twenty minutes, and I hate the books I'm reading, so I choose not to read."

This blew me away. Had no one ever told this child she didn't have to trudge through a book she didn't find fun or interesting? Had no one told her she could read something else? As her principal, I felt like I had failed her. As we walked to my office, we chatted about the people in her life, her favorite sports and her favorite animals. She had a whimsical mind and preferred books with main characters who were female but said she'd settle for reading a book about a boy "if it was really good." This little girl also said she'd like for the main character to be African-American, so she could read a book about someone who looked like her.

As we entered my office, I walked her over to my bookshelf, and I told her all the books on those shelves were mine. I hadn't read them all, but I was trying to. I asked her if she thought it might be okay if I showed her some of the books I had always loved. (Several also met her specifications.) I was holding out hope I could hook her with just the right book!

I pitched books like *Booked* and *Crossover* by Kwame Alexander, *Ruby Lee and Me* by Shannon Hitchcock, *Pax* by Sara Pennypacker, *Braced* by Alyson Gerber, *Ninth Ward* and *Bayou Magic* by Jewell Parker Rhodes, and several others. She watched very intensely, and I wasn't quite sure if any of the books were connecting. "Do any of those sound interesting?" I asked, watching as she leaned in to inspect each book. "What if they all sound good? What do I do then?"

I was taken aback but also really pleased because I had expected to have a much more challenging conversation. Instead, we sat there and talked about what she really liked about each book I recommended, and she ended up selecting *Booked* by Kwame Alexander and *Ruby Lee and Me* by Shannon Hitchcock.

As we walked back to class, she smiled, holding those books close to her chest. Before letting her go, I asked her for one favor. "Promise me that if you don't like these books, you'll return them right away," I said. "But if you do end up liking these books, share on the announcements about what you liked after you're finished reading them." She paused for a moment, thinking it over, and then she said, "I think I can do that."

> ## When your students walk into their classrooms at school, do they see their teachers and leaders as readers?

As my school's leader, I hold great responsibility. One thing I've learned about kids is they're always watching and listening. Another is they always want to be like the teachers and administrators they admire. That means setting powerful examples and showing our students we're readers—including book talks during the daily morning announcements, posting signs outside our classroom and office doors telling everyone what we're reading, and taking the time to read to and with students.

When your students walk into their classrooms at school, do they see their teachers and leaders as readers? Or do they see educators who talk about reading and tell students how to do it but rarely do it themselves?

The Teacher as Writer

In *Writing Toward Home*, Georgia Heard wrote:

> There are many times when I've felt that there was no poetry inside me, that I had nothing valuable to say. That the real writers were other people. It has taken me a while to believe that the way I feel each day, and the way I and others speak when we're least self-conscious, is where writing comes from. When we begin to speak in the language that is ours and tell our own stories and truth, we are surprised that this too is poetry.

Writing is difficult. Even now, after years of journaling, blogging, publishing books, and writing for students and teachers, we still feel limited by self-imposed and standards-based boundaries, countless distractions, and a shortage of this elusive thing called time. There are days when we might sit with a notebook in hand, pen suspended above a blank page, and yet still feel separated from the very act of writing. Those moments we begin to believe there is nothing worthwhile we have to say. We believe Georgia Heard's appraisal of poetry because it encapsulates everything we've come to understand about the writing process.

Most of the writing we completed in school was for someone else. The research paper on *Macbeth*, the response essay on *Tender is the Night*, the assigned writing prompt for the state test, the summaries of each short story we read, the book reports, and so on. None of those were for us. Opportunities to find writing, to locate poetry, and to identify our own self-awareness so that we could learn more about who we were as writers were almost nonexistent. We often wondered if we might have found a writing voice earlier if teachers had afforded us any of those opportunities.

Over time, we have learned that when we are not writing for others and refuse to acknowledge the internal editor that preys on superlative ideas, we spill our best writing onto a page. Our language is more precise and our descriptions more brilliant. We start exploring notions, distilling moments with vivid imagery and unearthing almost-forgotten memories. Instead of recognizing this as poetry—and it is, it always is—we substitute the word "poetry" with "writing": ". . . we are surprised that this too is writing." Georgia Heard's quote applies to all writing, whether it is the poetry we collect in our notebooks or the sentences we craft in essays. All of it is writing.

Learning to explore the world through language is a gift that we, as educators, can pass to our students. Before we can do that, though, we must become writers ourselves. Being a writer does not only mean being published in academic journals or widely-read magazines or that your name is printed boldly atop a book. It means you participate in the writing process and understand the frustrations and beauty that accompany writing. Not all of our writing is good. In fact, our writing notebooks and Google Drive accounts are filled with terrible first drafts. That however is where some of our best writing originates.

Two of the greatest voices in English/language arts are Donald Murray and Donald Graves. Both of these writers have had a profound impact on our writing lives as well as our understanding of what children are truly capable of in the classroom when it comes to reading and writing instruction. We often refer back to the words of Donald Murray, who said, "We write to discover what we want to say," knowing that the words we etch in our writing spaces will pave the way for better writing.

I (Todd) still remember when my college professor assigned us the task of writing and illustrating our own children's book. I was terrified. I loved writing, but I had never shared my writing with my own friends, much less strangers in a large college classroom.

I remember sitting for weeks, waiting to be inspired to write something, anything. One day the idea of writing about a little sprout of a tree, which never grew as large as the other trees, came to me. As I began to craft the story of little Spruce, the ideas began to flow. At first, they weren't great, and there was quite a bit of material to discard over the next forty-five drafts. But after choosing a friend for Spruce, an ant named Lucy, and shaping the conclusion to the story, I was off!

Turning that final copy into my professor was scary, but learning we would all read each other's stories was mortifying. After reading through the stories, we voted on which one moved us the most, and lo and behold, mine was selected! My professor helped me go through the process of getting my story and images copyrighted in the unlikely event that one day I would have it published. It was thrilling. I had never felt like anyone would find value in my words.

A few years later, I self-published my children's book, *Spruce & Lucy*, and began to use it as a teaching tool in my classroom. It's still around today in the classrooms of all my teachers on campus. I love reading it to students, and while I tell them the story is special to me, I never share that I am the author and illustrator. I read the story, we ask questions, and we share our thoughts on the characters and morals. Then I do the big reveal, and every time it blows their minds! We sit and talk about being scared to write, feeling like our words didn't matter, and what it's like to write a book.

We talk about finding your voice, how a book isn't finished in five minutes and with one draft, and we even talk about the copyright process. The kids eat it up, and it helps see that we're all writers at heart. That we all have a story begging to be told if we only give it voice. It's difficult, often scary, and it requires an enormous amount of work. But aren't those things the accomplishments we look back on with the most pride?

But writing isn't only about being successful and sharing those moments of triumph. If we're going to inspire our students and those in our field, we have to share our failures along with our successes.

As a writer, I (Travis) know failure quite well. Not all experiences seared my heart, but several have caused me to second-guess my writing abilities and criticize myself into a non-writerly lifestyle. The harshest experience came in college while I was writing my senior thesis. I attended a liberal arts school, and to graduate, literature majors were expected to write a lengthy thesis on an author of their choice, generate their own research question, and including no fewer than twenty documented sources within the paper. By nature, I am conversational and am rarely at a loss for words, so I was not fearful of the page requirement or the task itself. I was actually excited. We were also required to have a faculty advisor, someone in the literature department, to help guide our writing and thinking as we wrote our first piece of scholarship. I could not wait to begin.

> If we're going to inspire our students and those in our field, we have to share our failures along with our successes.

I had recently fallen in love with novels by Stephen King, amazed at his interesting stories, the symbols he chose, the intransigent protagonists, and the religious imagery evident throughout many of his books. *The Stand* became a favorite, and in my typical nerdy fashion, I began noting parallels between the novel and the Bible, even the Koran, which I had been studying in a college literature course. Confident in my choice for my thesis, I emailed the contemporary specialist in the literature department, excited to work with him and begin writing my paper. He emailed back immediately, saying he knew nothing about Stephen King and would not be able to work with me on this endeavor. I emailed another professor. Same response. I asked the entire literature department, and each individual turned me down. Little did I know that Stephen King's work was not considered scholarly by many in academia. His work was described as trivial and unimportant by one of the professors I emailed, and I was incredibly embarrassed to return to class once all of the professors had sent me their denials.

I did return to class, though, slinking to the back of the room and trying to hide. Rejection hurts. Writing rejection debilitates. I spoke with my senior thesis professor after class that day, and with her guidance and questioning, I decided to write my paper on Shakespeare's *Twelfth Night*. But it was already October. She assured me, in her calming way, that all would be fine if I started writing immediately and sought out help from an Elizabethan literature professor. Thankfully, he agreed to mentor my writing and the process began.

I wrote feverishly for weeks. My writing advisor helped, but the burden of the deadline weighed heavily. Meeting weekly, we discussed my ideas about *Twelfth Night*, sought meaningful ways to craft the various tenets of my argument, reviewed research and other theses related to my topic. He extended my thinking deeply during the weeks leading up to the due date. On the day the final draft of the paper was due, I carried the freshly printed copy to my senior thesis professor's office. She smiled when I handed it to her and wished me a wonderful Thanksgiving break.

When we returned from break, I received an email letting me know that I needed to see her immediately. Upon entering her office, she handed me my paper and told me she had reviewed it herself. I knew there were some mistakes, some redundancies, but I had no idea it was bad enough to merit the prolific comments and corrections on every page of the thirty-page draft I had submitted.

"Now that you have some time, I need you to go back and fix this. It is not ready to be reviewed by the department," she told me candidly.

I was speechless. Also crying. Writing is hard, and when you have spent hours crafting a thesis, believing it to be worthwhile, harsh feedback kills any drive to make it better. But I persevered, shaking off my doubt and the sting of some of the more acerbic comments written on my paper. Grabbing a notebook, I started to scribble ideas, deciding it would do me a world of good to write outside of my paper for a while. Eventually, ideas began to emerge, and they fit beautifully into my thesis. I hit "print" again. This time, when my professor reviewed the paper, it was accepted.

Writing about that experience never fails to evoke embarrassment. It is painful to recall a time when my writing was deemed unworthy, possibly even mocked. Today, when I work with writers, I think of this story. If I want to move students to write, I have to let them. I have to, as Don

Graves mentioned, receive their work and listen. Notice what students are trying to do and guide them as they work toward that goal. Because I have participated in the writing process, I know what it feels like to be daunted by a blank page, hurt by criticism, and inspired by scribbling.

Writer and teacher Barry Lane pushes writers to consider this,

Just start to scribble.
This is what I tell students—just write.
But we must write, too.
And we must understand the process.

Authentic writing takes place when students, as Barry Lane says, just start to scribble. With the simple act of putting pen to paper and writing from deep within, beautiful stories begin to pour onto the pages. This type of writing is not bound by rubrics or teacher-created criteria. It is whimsical, joyful, and delightful. As educators, sometimes like our students, all we have to do is start to scribble. And like our students, we must participate in the writing process.

The Writer's Notebook

All writers need a place to hold their thinking. When students respond to quick writes, work with poems that are burgeoning inside of them, craft memoirs, and collect sentences and words that are beautiful and well-constructed, they need a place to hold those ideas. A writing notebook serves that purpose. Whether it is a tangible notebook or digital file, a place to capture thinking is important in the life of a writer.

We ask students to keep writing notebooks, so all of their thinking is collected in one place. Most days, the writing portion of class begins with a quick write response to a poem with the sole objective being that the student pours out his or her reactions, emotions, and thoughts on the page. These are collected within the pages of their writer's notebooks. What this has provided is a space that students can easily refer back to in order to grow future writing pieces and seeds of ideas that are only beginning to grow into something more.

As adults we too see the value of having something like a writer's notebook. The physical space of a notebook becomes a wonderful reference for partially-formed thinking that budded from quick writes and reading responses, as well as the sentences they crafted as they composed the beautiful stories that live within them.

Writing with, from, and alongside Mentor Texts

When we ask students to generate writing, we want them to write with passion and conviction, composing work that they are willing to spend time crafting, revising, and polishing. There are moments when students lack inspiration, and they complain that they have nothing to say, that there is no story thumping on their hearts. The use of mentor texts give students a place to grow their writing. Simply put, mentor texts provide a starting point.

> There are moments when students lack inspiration, and they complain that they have nothing to say, that there is no story thumping on their hearts.

A *mentor text* is a piece of writing that authors use to guide their thinking, providing them with structural help, sentences, vocabulary, paragraphing, and style. Any beginner needs a place to start, and with the right resources, students can write beautiful poems, essays, and short stories. Writers need to read and study different types of mentor texts to guide their own writing. They are useful, and here is how we infuse them into our work with student writers.

Every year, students are asked to craft a memoir (for more information about the power of memoir and the beautiful effect it has on students, see Chapter 8). As a group, we study a section of *The Glass Castle* by Jeannette Walls, a piece of *Bad Boy* by Walter Dean Myers, a segment of *My Beloved World* by Sonia Sotomayor, and Travis's personal memoir, *Change Can Be Difficult* (available in Chapter 7). We also read student examples from previous years together and ask students to identify the sections that speak to them personally, the stories that resonate with them, and the qualities that make these pieces memorable.

We also ask them questions to nudge their thinking as they begin to write their own.

"What story from your past, one that has changed you or affected you, would you like to tell?"

Then, "Which of the mentor texts has a structure that you would like to use to tell your story? Which of the structures will convey your thinking the best?"

As students begin crafting their own memoirs, we use individual conferences to guide students as they think about their own stories, asking them to identify the mentor text (in this case, one of the memoirs) that they will use to guide the writing and structure of theirs.

Devon was moved by a student memoir sample that we read and studied as a group. The structure and story resonated with him. His memoir took shape in his notebook. It was inspiring to see him use a mentor text to guide his writing.

Student Memoir Mentor Text

My memoir

When I was 5 my Aunt and my Uncle got a divorce. I had never went through the experience of a divorce before and I thought that the divorce wouldn't change anything big. I didn't realize how wrong I could be.

***

My cousins were 11, 13, and 14. Even though they were older than me, they would still take Anna and I with them to do stuff if we wanted to. We would go everywhere together and play outside. Zack, Collin, and Seth would go with us to ride dirt bikes at our house over at the sawmill. My Aunt and Uncle owned a Pontoon and we would sometimes go out on the boat. When we weren't out doing something, we would be a Maw's and Paw's driving the golf cart in the pastor or around the loop. On hot summer days, we would go to the creek and play. And on others we would play on the tire swing in the yard.

One day we went to Maw's house and she said that my Uncle and my Aunt had had conflict and that she had left to stay with one of her friends until they could sort things out. A few long weeks later, we received news from my Aunt saying that she had had a deliberation with my uncle and they had decided that the best thing to do was to get a divorce. She said that they would have the divorce made final next month while they decided what to do with their things. They had been having a few minor problems but I was too young to realize that they were having much more of a problem. We were all in shock that they were getting a divorce and didn't know what was going to happen. After about a year later we had pretty much settled back down from the divorce and my Aunt had taken with her a lot of their stuff so they were just getting settled back down when she called and said that she wanted my cousins to permanently move in with her. My cousins meant the world to my Uncle. He had been letting them stay with her for two weeks and him two weeks in the summer but during the school year they would stay with him to go to school because all of their friends were here. He really did love them but she didn't seem to understand that so she got them to move to Boone with her. My Uncle tried his hardest to get them back but he couldn't seem to get her to understand that he loved them. He was devastated after they left. He tried to stay in contact with them but she wouldn't let them so he eventually got excluded from their world. Collin, Zack, and Seth really tried to get their Mom to let them come back to see us but she feared that they would then want to stay with my Uncle instead of her so she would not let them. My family has moved on but I think that there will always be a car that she put on us.

Devon's Memoir

In addition to a memoir, we also study poetry, a genre that works with all content areas. Students gravitate to poems because of the content and structural differences. Many times, we give poems to students and ask them to paste them inside their notebooks. Then, students spend time reading and reflecting and writing beside these poems. Encountering poetry is critical in the life of a writer because poetry is a genre that touches all other types of writing. Writers speak to an audience through metaphor and simile, personification, and allusion. These terms are often relegated to poetry units in language arts classrooms, but they are alive in every other content area. They breathe life into understanding, especially as students massage their fledgling understanding of more abstract concepts.

Using poetry as a mentor text breathes life into writing.

Julie entered my (Travis) class as a student who despised writing, but studying a poem from *Crank* by Ellen Hopkins caused her writing life to explode. She began playing with structure, building story, and above all else, she began *writing*. Her writing life was never the same.

Regardless of content area, students can write with, from, and alongside mentor texts. If we want students to write, we have to give them places to start. Writing is a daunting task. It requires focus, revision, and inspiration. Consider the places in your content area where poetry or other mentor texts would engage students in writing. Paste those pieces of writing inside their notebooks. Find those mentor texts, give students time to paste them inside their notebooks, and watch as they create thoughtful pieces of writing based on the mentors you shared with them.

Notebook Time

About two years ago, I (Travis) was conferencing with students, asking them about editorials they were writing. Students had chosen topics of interest and were meticulously crafting their pieces in response to feedback I had recently provided. They were excited to share their essays with the world, but after several conferences, I noticed a trend in their responses to my questions.

"So, tell me about your piece," I said to each student, listening to them describe their writing and read sections that they were struggling to craft.

"What do you need from me?" I concluded, eager for their feedback.

Each student I spoke with was enjoying the writing, but they were curious about when they would be able to return to pieces they had started earlier in the year. There were poems, short stories, essays, and quick writes that they wanted to return to. "Will we be able to return to those?" they asked.

In response to their concern, I began implementing notebook time in my class.

> I encourage students to experiment with language, style, structure, and genre during notebook time.

Several days a week, students are given time to go back into their notebooks and find pieces of writing that they want to continue building or craft new ones. I encourage students to experiment with language, style, structure, and genre during notebook time. As the year continues, students become more confident in their writing and begin consulting mentor texts on their own. Below is a sample from Emily's notebook. After reading *The Running Dream* by Wendelin Van Draanen, she wanted to begin writing her own story based on big ideas in the novel. Emily is also fond of the outdoors and after reading *Majestic*, a poem by Kwame Alexander, she decided to use her love of nature to write a poem about a bumblebee.

In addition to writing, I allow and encourage students to create illustrations in their notebooks. If there is a poem or story that would be enhanced by a drawing, I allow them to use notebook time to craft it. Emily's illustration was born after ten minutes of notebook time one morning. Considering the amount of writing she has produced this year, an illustration is a beautiful complement to anything she writes.

Notebook time is a wonderful feature in an English/language arts classroom, but it can have a place inside of other content areas. When students have time to "play" with elements of a content area, engagement increases. When students are whimsical with their writing, future writing becomes deeper and more complex. We encourage you to find a place in your curriculum for this no-strings attached, playful, and often idiosyncratic type of writing. Students will take risks with form and content when the stakes are removed, and they are able to create pieces from a place of joy and delight. We encourage you to gift them with this opportunity. You will not be disappointed.

It's Our Responsibility

In the end, it's our responsibility as educators to make sure our personal lives are rich with diverse reading and writing opportunities. And, more importantly, that we're sharing those experiences with our students.

They need to see us as readers. They need to see us as writers. They need to know learning is messy, hard, and filled with mistakes and struggles, but the rewards of reading a book that breaks your heart or writing your truth are powerful moments that can't be replicated anywhere else.

THINGS TO THINK ABOUT AND TWEET

How can we inspire those around us to want
to read and write more?

What have you had to change in your
personal or professional life to make more
time for reading and writing for yourself?

What barriers stand in your way?

What is your biggest fear of sharing your
reading and writing life with others?

How can we discuss with
students the benefits of a
healthy, voluminous, reading life?

How are you taking the time to discover the
reading interests your students have?

What do your students enjoy writing about?

What can you do to ensure that students are writing about the things that are meaningful to them?

Are you providing daily independent reading time not only for your students but also for you?

When is the best time for you to write?

What story is currently thumping in your heart? Is this a story you can take to your writing notebook?

What is a piece of writing that you can share with your students?

How might blogging, daily writing, or publishing a piece of writing help you as a teacher of readers and writers?

#SparksInTheDark

Life is a matter of choices, and every choice you make, makes you.

—John Maxwell

Chapter 5

If We Let Them

MAKING CHOICES IS AN inevitable part of life. Depending on circumstances, the process can be overwhelming, exciting, frustrating, and empowering. In most situations, the act of making choices for ourselves keeps us moving forward and helps us persist through struggles. Whether it's choosing the car we want to drive, what color to paint the kitchen, or where to go for dinner, choice matters. Especially when you're an educator trying to grow readers and writers. Think about it. Enjoyment, interest, and fascination are what lie at the heart of reading and writing, and those responses simply cannot be dictated by an outside force. Sure, students can be required to read specific texts or write particular essays, but if they're not intrigued, captivated, or truly engaged, it's just an academic exercise. To shape students into lifelong readers and writers, we must relinquish some of our control and allow kids the freedom to choose the books and topics that speak to them.

We see significant numbers of students leaving our classrooms with a real aversion to reading. They move on to higher grades, community colleges, and universities without developing any kind of personal reading or writing life. What is happening in our schools to encourage this attitude? What demonizes reading, causing students to abhor what so many people consider pleasurable? And when is this love of reading lost?

From personal experience, I (Travis) know students left my classroom for years with a disdain for reading. They enjoyed me as a teacher and praised my commitment to their learning, but no one developed a rich reading life. When I think about how I required students to read the books I selected, I realize the massive amount of time they missed reading what they wanted to read.

Every summer, several weeks before the school year began, a coworker and I would plan our entire year, marking the weeks we would spend teaching Shakespeare, Bradbury, grammar, vocabulary, writing, and much more. After all, we were the experts. We had spent years developing our teaching craft, and without a doubt, we were adept at reading and explaining complex texts. The first day of school, I explained the rigorous expectations outlined in my detailed syllabus. Students would be reading challenging literature, studying grammar, discussing and memorizing a massive amount of vocabulary words, and writing several essays in response to the texts we would be analyzing. It would be fun. In addition to these incredible requirements, students would be completing independent reading projects. They were to choose one book each grading quarter, read it outside of class, and be prepared to turn in their reading project on a designated date. Out of fear and in compliance, most students completed the project. Today I am ashamed of this approach and the teacher-centric classroom I created.

My classroom was devoid of authentic student choice and voice. It was a culture of compliance instead of joy and discovery. Although I believe in holding students to high expectations—and requiring that they read and write prodigiously—those expectations should not inhibit students voice.

When teachers allow students to choose their own books, assignments, and the ways they will demonstrate mastery, it sends a clear message to students that we value their voices. When I limited the voice of my students to one independent reading assignment each grading quarter, I made it clear that I only valued their contributions when a grade was attached and independent reading only mattered if it was completed outside of school.

In her book, *In the Middle*, Nancie Atwell discusses the controversial nature of student choice in the classroom. Even today, well into the twenty-first century, student choice sparks debate. But why? It seems strange, this notion that student choices are avoided and even scoffed at by quite a number of educators.

Curious, we asked some of our colleagues what they think about allowing student choice in their classrooms. Here are some of the answers we received:

- Students will not select challenging books if left to their own devices.
- Children do not have the cognitive development necessary to choose.
- Choices are "okay" if students are guided through the process.
- Limiting students to two to four choices works best, especially in a rigorous course.
- Student choice is only provided when students are working on a project.

Of all of these responses, the one we agree with most is the idea that there's a need to guide students through the process. With guidance and opportunity, students' choices become more academic, focused, and challenging.

Several years ago, when I (Travis) was starting this journey of incorporating reading and writing workshops into my language arts classes, I was blessed to teach Anna, a voracious reader whose experiences in

ELAR classes had been less than stellar. Although she had laser focus in school and was determined to maintain an "A" average in all her coursework, Anna admitted, on a reading interest inventory, that she found language arts class frustrating. "When teachers choose the books I read, and we all have to read them at the same pace, it discourages me. I could read four books by the time we finish one," she told me during a reading conference. I believed her.

If Anna had been in my class a year earlier, she would have started the year with *The Outsiders*, moved on to *Fahrenheit 451*, segued into *Hamlet*, and finished up with *To Kill a Mockingbird*, *The Book Thief*, or a series of short stories I loved reading with my students. She also would have completed an independent reading assignment each grading period. Because of Anna's personality and intrinsic motivation, she would have excelled in my class, seeking to understand each text, writing her heart out on essay tests and striving to ace quizzes (yes, I was that teacher). But the year I taught Anna, I made a significant shift in my teaching practices, implementing a free-choice, independent reading environment where students were responsible for selecting the texts they read for ninety percent of their ELA experience. I owe all of Anna's success to that paradigm shift.

Teachers have told me repeatedly that students will not select challenging books if they are in a reading workshop environment. At one time, I would have agreed, believing in the value of my teacher-centric curriculum as opposed to the student-centric curriculum I have adopted and continue to implement year after year. Anna's reading list for that year included more than forty books, including *And the Mountains Echoed* by Khaled Hosseini, *To Kill a Mockingbird* by Harper Lee, and *The Nightingale* by Kristin Hannah.

Choice is powerful. And it was not only Anna who challenged herself as a reader and, ultimately, a thinker. Kyler became an expert in Stephen King literature, reading more than ten books by the master of horror. Alex, whose reading life had been limited to overused worksheets, broke free from his "low-level" reading label and devoured *Unbroken* by Laura

Hillenbrand, *The Book Thief* by Markus Zusak, and *Fahrenheit 451* by Ray Bradbury, reading more than thirty books across seven genres, all of which were above his supposed reading level.

Choice is powerful.

How? Because he chose to.

Students are empowered when they have freedom to choose the books they read. Some of our critics have condemned our classrooms as unfocused, our guidelines nebulous, our expectations unchallenging. We realize that our methodology is, in ways, unorthodox to some. And while it may appear that there are no guidelines and expectations in our classrooms, the opposite is actually true. Choice is a critical piece of our instruction; however, we promote classrooms where teachers lead students to a deeper awareness of their reading abilities through choice. Across the year, we nudge students toward more challenging literature, encouraging them to enhance their reading lives by reading voluminously and widely across many genres, styles, and authors. Giving choice is not a free-for-all, as some critics have asserted. It increases the utility of the teacher, providing a golden opportunity to guide to students toward books that will pique their interest and challenge their thinking. It also means that teachers do not take the one-novel-for-the-entire-class approach to teaching literature because that increases the risk of losing readers.

I (Todd) remember so clearly the novels that were assigned to me in high school. Not because I actually read them, but because I hated being told what to read. CliffsNotes was my best friend, as was the case with many of my peers. We were handed a novel, told to read it, and be ready to answer a few multiple-choice questions the next day in class.

With no interest in the characters and no care or concern for the plot, I was completing an assignment in the quickest way possible with the smallest amount of effort necessary. Looking back, I can remember being assigned *Of Mice and Men* or *The Scarlet Letter* or *A Midsummer*

Night's Dream. But can I tell you what happened in those books? Can I explain to you why the characters made the choices they did? What the author was trying to convey through telling their stories? No, sadly, I cannot. And I would be bold enough to assume that many of you reading this book also can't remember many of the classics you were assigned in high school either.

I have always had a hard-headed personality. If you tell me to do something—or even better, not to do something—I will probably do the opposite. When it came to reading, I hated having a teacher select my material. Did she not know my interests as a reader were different from hers? Did he not understand I didn't care for novels in that style? Don't get me wrong—I work in an elementary school where I see my students introduced to characters and storylines and authors they would have never chosen on their own, but through the guidance of a class read-aloud, they fell in love. The point I'm making is that choice must always be part of the equation.

The stories we've shared above might be from language arts, but we tell you these stories to remind every educator about the power of student choice in the classroom. When given options, students will push themselves.

Does that mean that every child will take advantage of the opportunity of choice and run with it? No. If you've been in education for very long at all, you know that not every child makes the choices we are trying to guide them to. But it doesn't mean we stop. We would much rather see students in classrooms where teachers are struggling with getting one or two students to choose a book that works for them instead of entire classrooms forced to read only what is selected by the teacher.

THINGS TO THINK ABOUT AND TWEET

How have you given your students choice and seen great results come from it?

How has your administration given you a choice in your learning? If it hasn't, in what areas would you like to have more choice?

How can we be prepared for those who might speak against us giving our students more control in the classroom?

#SparksInTheDark

Literature is no one's private ground, literature is common ground; let us trespass freely and fearlessly and find our own way for ourselves.

—Virginia Woolf

Chapter 6

Choice in All Classrooms

WHAT DO WE DO in our other subject areas? We can't just be educators who create these fantastic reading opportunities only in language arts classrooms. Here are a few ideas that we have come up with to help begin the conversation of reading choice in all classrooms:

Social Studies

Social studies works beautifully as a humanities course, and it's an ideal place to use a reading and writing workshop to engage students in thinking about the past and how it connects to the present. It is important to remember that a teacher's job is to promote thinking, using texts as a guide. In social studies, texts blend seamlessly with the conversation, writing, and projects that enhance the quality of a humanities course. Choices are a bit limited in social studies because the course is content-based, not skills-based as in language arts, but there is plenty of room for student choice.

I (Travis) am not a lecturer. At all. I prefer discovery learning but understand that lecturing is a component of most classes, and at times, teachers must designate a time during class to disseminate critical pieces of information. It is not my style, though. Jim Burke, a high school English teacher and author of *The English Teacher's Companion*, described the three acts that organize his English class. I have found this three-act approach works wonderfully in my social studies classes. When introducing a new concept or idea, I ask students to read a text. These texts may include videos, articles, selections from books in my classroom library, a primary-source document, or a quote. Other times, I may pose a question to my students, inviting them into a large or small group conversation focused on a big idea housed within that question. Throw out an idea such as love or hatred, and everyone has a story, a connection, a thread that unites them to the big idea.

For example, we once discussed the notions of liberty and justice. Our starting point was the Pledge of Allegiance. We talked about its vocabulary, and I posted pieces of chart paper around the room with key words—*justice, liberty, allegiance, indivisible,* and *for all*—written at the top. Students participated in a gallery walk, writing their thinking on the pieces of chart paper. They could pose questions, answer the questions of others, write their opinions, talk about a book, short story, poem, or recent event related to the overall ideas. They were also challenged to complete this task silently, so they could better focus on their own thinking.

Once they finished with the gallery walk, I asked them to choose one of the ideas and write about it for several minutes, answering the following question: When you consider this idea, what comes to mind? Broadening the question and focusing on their choices and their thinking encouraged a different type of classroom environment. I was not concerned about the meaning of a word, finding the main idea, or highlighting supporting details or evidence for an answer. I simply wanted to know what they were thinking.

After this part of the lesson, we moved to another piece, one that involved more opportunities for student choice. I collected links to several videos, ones I felt would create a surge of conversation in small- and large-group discussion. I placed these links, a total of six, on a document and told students they were to watch at least three. At the end, they had to respond to questions that related the videos to liberty and justice. Afterward, I asked them to write a letter to a person or entity, explaining one of the videos, and offering suggestions for a worldwide, country-wide, or local change. I encourage students to write letters often because it requires written expression, a focused idea, supporting details, and an understanding of an author's craft. I required students to find someone to mail the letter to, such as an exact mailing address or professional email, but I did not require that they be mailed. If students wanted them mailed or emailed, I assisted them.

> If students own something,
> they will work hard to choose
> that just-right arrangement
> of words and images.

Choice begets ownership. If students own something, they will work hard to choose that just-right arrangement of words and images. At the end of each project, we took the time to ask students to give themselves a grade and argue the reason they should receive that grade. We also allowed them to offer feedback by asking them if they thought this assignment should be repeated with other classes. The freedom they had to choose was listed, by every student, as a reason to keep the assignment going. Choice is powerful.

Mathematics

As we have stated before in this book, literacy is the cornerstone of every subject. Including math. If children can't read and read with fluency and comprehension, they will struggle throughout all the other content areas.

Regardless of the age you teach, there are countless opportunities to incorporate high-quality picture books into mathematics instruction. To provide students with stories that speak to concepts they're currently learning. And better yet? You can have students create their own math problems using the characters from the stories you've read together.

Asking questions such as, "If these changes had been made, what do you think might have happened?" is also helpful.

As you give this a try, remember that students thrive when given choices. In the math classroom, there are a number of opportunities to give students choices for how they might solve a particular problem. If there's more than one way to solve it, allow your students to choose. For decades, we've told students there's only one way to get a correct answer, but in reality, there are often many. When you allow students to choose their own path to the answer, they typically want to prove to you how they got there and how they understand the material. As a result, they are much more likely to master the material and retain the information.

When I (Todd) moved from teaching traditionally to using a flipped, project-based style of teaching, I quit handing out worksheets with test-formatted questions. Instead, I focused on generating activities for my students that would have them getting their hands dirty in the learning.

I had seen firsthand the value of providing students with choices in their learning— guiding them, but giving them some freedom as well.

One of my favorite activities was teaching them about fractions. Instead of just handing out different mathematical questions involving fractions, we built an entire project around the concept. The thing my students complained about the most was school lunches. Our project was to use the USDA's website to build a new lunch menu. Abiding by the regulations, students had to look at the recipes and nutrition facts and plan a dream menu for one day. They had to provide the exact amount of each food item and explain how it would feed all of the students at the school, while also including the total cost. Students then drafted proposals, which they also had to present to the head of the food service department in hopes that their menu would be selected to be implemented at the school. Excitement could not be contained as students worked their hearts out, creating a product that would affect the real world: the cafeteria. When the winning menu was finally chosen, it did of course include french fries and ice cream: two staples on every child's dream menu.

The math and collaboration they learned from this activity exceeded anything I could have imparted with a simple worksheet or packet. Yes, it put a lot of the control in their hands, but that's what they wanted! Our kids need to earn their own learning and feel like what they're doing matters.

Math class doesn't have to be that class period where the teacher shows how to complete a math equation, and students go on their own and practice and solve similar math equations. Choice is important everywhere.

> Providing time for children to read in every classroom shows the students just how important reading is.

And what else is important even in a math classroom? Independent reading time. Providing time for children to read in every classroom shows the students just how important reading is and that, yes, your math teacher reads too.

Science

And what about science? So often much of our science instruction takes place through lab experiments. And that's exactly how science should be. Students will always learn best when they can learn through hands-on, inquisitive, and experiential learning. But instead of limiting ourselves to labs, why not try to incorporate more reading and writing skills into our science classes?

At the elementary level, picture books about the scientific process or famous scientists are a wonderful way to capture students' curiosity. You can have students write brief essays comparing what was presented in the book and what actually happened when their class conducted the experiment.

What if we had students within their science classes take a poem or short story that deals with a current topic of study? Students then could use those poems and short stories as mentor texts to create their own or further dissect the topic at hand.

Incorporating reading or writing skills into a science classroom doesn't have to be drastic or complicated. And if you don't know where to begin, reach out to your school's ELAR teachers, your librarian, your district specialists, or other educators online. Don't let your fear or your lack of experience stop you from providing the best learning possible for your students.

> Student choice is synonymous with student engagement, in both reading and writing. It's my responsibility as an educator to invite, nurture, and sustain every student's engagement with literature.
>
> —Nancie Atwell

Embracing the Workshop Model

Giving children the freedom to make their own choices is scary. We have had these same fears. What if they don't try? What if they choose wrong? What if I'm not in control?

But what if they do try? What if they choose correctly? What if you not being in control is even better for your students? We can't fear the poor choices of a few and allow those to define the choices we make for the whole.

Providing students with choices should no longer be voluntary. It should be a requirement in every classroom. Because how will we ever value the voices of our children if we're not allowing them to have any kind of say in their learning experiences?

> You can become a teacher of more
> than just students whose warm
> bodies fill the room each day.

We are convinced that a workshop classroom, one that embraces the workshop spirit, is the only way to fully engage students in conversations about books and writing and to enhance their abilities to analyze and evaluate different forms of literature. We have seen engagement increase exponentially when students have the freedom to choose their own reading materials, select their own writing topics, and collaborate with their classmates to expand their thinking. You can become a teacher of more than just students whose warm bodies fill the room each day. When we value our students, listen to them, and give them a voice within their classrooms, we will learn about the conditions necessary for a successful learning environment.

Listening to students is key. And while teachers can glean valuable knowledge from reading all kinds of literature, educational research, and the latest on adolescent brain development, none of that will ever supersede the insights you can gain from conversations with your students. Talk with them, ask questions about their lives, their likes and dislikes, the books they like, the dreams they have. We love Penny Kittle's *Write Beside Them* and Donalyn Miller's *The Book Whisperer*. These works are rich with inspiration and guidance, and they are starting points, to help you navigate the uncertain waters of the classroom. The greatest knowledge we have gained has come from our students, and these deeper understandings will be held in our hearts forever.

Coleen

If we let them, students will write. During writing workshops, I (Travis) have watched students linger over paragraphs and sentences, searching for the perfect words to express their thoughts. They long to tell stories, both personal and imaginative, and they need a teacher to give them the time and space it requires.

Coleen fell in love with books by Ellen Hopkins. *Crank* was one of her favorites, and during notebook time one day, she decided to use that novel as a mentor text, writing her own story while using Hopkins' structure. It was her intense focus that caught my attention, and as she feverishly wrote, I looked over her shoulder. A story in verse was taking shape, and it was amazing. I prompted her to tell me about this story, and she explained that she loved how the novel was written in poetry and wanted to experiment with the style. The powerful element in her writing was that she had had no instruction in this style of writing. She masterfully paired dialogue with an internal monologue, and a narrative took shape quickly. All I did was give her time to write.

Easton

If we let them, students will read. Many students enter our classrooms, convinced they are nonreaders. Never before are they placed in a classroom where time is set aside daily for independent reading. Several students have even admitted they await the moment a teacher would take independent reading time away from them and pass out a class novel, removing their opportunities to select their own books.

Easton's reading life had been limited to class-wide novels and teacher-focused conversation, and my independent reading expectation was cumbersome for him to think about. On the third day of school, he approached me with *The Shining* by Stephen King, a book he had checked out from the public library.

"May I read this during class?" he asked.

"Absolutely," I replied. "But I'd like to know why you chose that particular book."

It was a copious novel, but his determination to read it was evident.

"I just want to read one of Stephen King's books," he said.

It took Easton more than a month to finish *The Shining*, but he was always engaged during reading conferences, and when he wrote about this book, his writing was lively. He spoke eloquently about characters and their ambitions, and after several months and several other King novels, Easton became our resident expert in the horror genre. Later he abandoned King to explore Lemony Snicket and some historical fiction, but he found his way back to the genre that had initially captivated him. Having time to read was a critical factor in his transformation. Without time to read, students will not be able to explore genres they might fall in love with or find an author to whom they develop an allegiance. All I did was let Easton read. And read he did.

Everly

If we let them, students will choose challenging books. It was Teri Lesesne's seminal *Reading Ladders* that helped me understand the importance of building bridges between where students are and where we'd like them to be as readers. Giving students reading choices is empowering, and when they know they have ownership, they will take it seriously. When students have the power to choose their own books, they may start with what we view as simplistic reads; however, as students read more, they naturally begin to seek more challenging books, searching for the novels that will stimulate deeper thinking. They will build a sophisticated reading ladder, and at the end of the year, you will celebrate their accomplishments with them.

Everly admitted she was not as strong of a reader as she wanted to be. Her interest in reading was minimal, but if she had to read, she would. She started the year with books of 100 pages or less, but after a while, she began searching for books that would challenge her as a thinker. In reading conferences, she would talk about how she wished the story would develop more, so I suggested more developed books. She read *Noggin* by John Corey Whaley and *Winger* by Andrew Smith, identifying these as the types of stories she had been looking for. Her reading life took a detour when she read *The Burn Journals* by Brent Runyon, a memoir about an adolescent boy who set himself aflame and, as a result, had to endure the agony of multiple skin grafts. During various reading conferences, she explained that these books taught her about people and showed her a side of humanity that she had not seen before. Her reading life included more than thirty books, but I was most impressed when I saw her reading *All the Light We Cannot See* by Anthony Doerr, which won the Pulitzer for Fiction in 2015. I did not assign any of those novels; Everly chose them. And she chose challenging books because she wanted to read them.

Julie

If we let them, students will teach us, and our classrooms will change. Our lessons will come alive for students because we have included them by the simple act of listening and allowing choice. But we have to let them have a voice, and we have to give them a platform within our classrooms. If we let them, they will show us the type of learning environment that will work for them. Each group is unique, and our knowledge of those groups must inform the lessons we use. If we let them, students will tell us what works and what doesn't, what they want to learn, and the questions they have. If we let them, they will teach us how to be better educators.

> If we let them, students will teach us,
> and our classrooms will change.

Julie was always quiet and compliant. She completed all of her work on time and never complained about an assignment or book selection presented to her. She had a smile on her face, a "Yes, sir" on her lips, and the type of personality that wants to please the teacher. But something changed in Julie when I (Todd) allowed the students to form book clubs and select any novel they wanted to read together. Julie partnered with another student, and they selected *Towers Falling* by Jewell Parker Rhodes. After finishing it, Julie came up to me with tears in her eyes, and I asked her what was wrong.

"I've never read a book like that before," she said. "It broke me. I chose it because I wasn't alive for 9/11, and now after reading it, I don't know how I could have handled living through that. Thank you for letting me choose a book with no conditions. Would it be okay if I do a book talk and share this book with others in the class?"

Of course, I said yes, and after her passionate talk, eleven of my other twenty-three students read the book.

> When we let our students experience
> a little freedom, even when that freedom
> exists within parameters we set,
> we find that is so often
> when they educate us.

Our successes as teachers and administrators hinge on our willingness to let students be our teachers. And while we are giving them the time and space to read and write and talking about reading and writing, we must keep the conversation flowing, asking thought-provoking questions and nudging them in the right direction. Under these conditions, students will read with fervor and write with conviction, developing unique identities as readers and writers. They will challenge themselves and seek opportunities to increase the rigor of their reading lives and about the genres they choose to write. They will engage in conversations with their peers about books and writing and collaborate on ways to make their essays and stories come to life.

Their journey won't always be perfect. It won't always be pretty. There will be days of struggle, doubt, frustration, anxiety, and fear that they are accomplishing nothing we're trying to teach them or that they might not pass the test we're required to give. But when we let our students experience a little freedom, even when that freedom exists within parameters we set, we find that is so often when they educate us.

But only if we let them.

THINGS TO THINK ABOUT AND TWEET

In what ways can we encourage more choice within different subject areas?

How can you support your colleagues in providing insight and resources?

What child have you seen impacted by a different kind of teaching style?

#SparksInTheDark

People who are skilled at dialogue do their best to make it safe for everyone to add their meaning to the shared pool—even ideas that at first glance appear controversial, wrong, or at odds with their own beliefs. Now, obviously they don't agree with every idea; they simply do their best to ensure that all ideas find their way into the open.

—Kerry Patterson

Chapter 7

Critical Conversations

TALK IS A POWERFUL tool. It is during dialogue that we argue ideas, build new ones, extend our thinking, and grapple with the words and phrases that will enhance an argument. Monologues can be helpful tools as well. When engaged in an interior conversation, one that is alive with personality and vigor, we maneuver through tough issues and questions that plague us. Conversation is a beautiful part of instruction and an element that has the power to transform thinking and enhance the quality of a reading and writing life.

I (Travis) talk to my students all the time. I am concerned about them (What teacher isn't?), but I am also curious about what they are thinking. My questions range from general inquiries about their day to the deep connections they make to books and writing. During the twenty minutes of independent reading that take place at the beginning of each language arts class period, I check in with students about their reading lives and simply listen to what they have to say about the books they are reading. I try not to burden our conversations with technical vocabulary. I listen and nudge them further with questions that will build their thinking about reading.

I keep a notebook for each language arts class, and within that notebook, one page, front and back, is dedicated to the reading life of each child. This notebook is the place where I capture pieces of the conversations I have with them. Some of the questions I ask are:

- What are you thinking about as you read this book?
- What do you notice?
- What is the problem?
- Are you finding yourself reading this book faster, slower, or the same as other books?
- Where do you see yourself in this book? Are you seeing the story through a character's eyes, or are you standing on the side, watching the story unfold?
- From what point of view is the story told? Is that effective for this story?
- What is your plan once you have finished this book?

I do my best to have conversations that readers have while they are reading. There are no worksheets or irrelevant projects that interfere with the reading. It is a simple act of reading and responding and thinking. When we are finished talking, I let them return to their books.

These are not the only conversations students have about what they're reading. I often ask students to turn and talk with their tablemates, or find another person in the class with whom they have not spoken, and discuss:

- What's currently happening in their books
- A problem the characters are facing

These conversations are immensely important in the reading and writing classrooms, but it shouldn't stop there. We should discuss reading with students in every subject area.

> **We should discuss reading with students in every subject area.**

Even in the mathematics classroom, I (Todd) asked my students to talk or write about their learning process. For years, I thought that was the most asinine thing I'd ever heard. I couldn't see the value and figured it was silly to waste time writing when I needed them to actually be solving problems.

Then I attended a workshop on incorporating writing into mathematics instruction. At this workshop, the presenter asked the educators in attendance to solve a math problem. But not just to work the equation and write the answer. No, we had to write out every step and explain it with words on the page instead of numbers. Talk about difficult! I struggled to find the correct terms to explain the process the learner would use. And that's when it hit me. That is why my students, even in a math class, needed to be talking and writing.

The moment I returned to my classroom, my teaching changed. And guess what else changed? The vocabulary my students were using and the depth at which they were able to explain their thinking. One of my favorite activities was to have my students work with a partner. One person held the pencil and wasn't allowed to talk while the other sat on their hands and had to explain using only words. It was quite the task to get the student with the pencil to do exactly what the other student explained. If she said, "Write a one on top of the six," the partner with the pencil literally had to write a one overlaid on a six. The exercise was as frustrating as it was funny, and my students began to understand how mathematics is about much more than simply solving equations. They learned the value of using precise language. By sitting and talking about what we were doing, why we were doing it, and taking the time to explain our processing, they gained a deeper and better understanding of the material they were studying.

We will forever be supporters of talk in the classroom, especially in this digital age, because person-to-person interaction continues to build deeper thinking.

Conversations That Lead to Inquiry

Like language arts, my (Travis) social studies classes are always astir with talk. I use a problem-based learning (PBL) model for social studies, thinking about the course in terms of the humanities instead of history. Because of this mindset and model, conversation is always happening. It is during this talk time that students develop deeper ideas about the content and generate thought-provoking questions. I am not a lecturer, and even though I find many lectures interesting, including ones about authors, books, fascinating scientific topics, and issues of great concern, that is not a model I often follow. I have used it in the past, but without any guarantee that they are actually listening, I have gravitated to a more student-centered model. This is by no means a criticism of lecture-based teaching. I am merely hoping to start a serious conversation about the power of talk in our classrooms.

Let me tell you a story.

We began a unit on world exploration. Instead of introducing the unit with information on different explorers, their routes, the conflicts they encountered, and what they discovered, I introduced a concept—exploration through inquiry. This approach naturally lent itself to conversation among my students. On pieces of chart paper, placed in the middle of each group, I asked students to write the word "exploration." Around this word, they wrote down the different ways people explore. The chart paper—a tool I use frequently—served as a place to capture their thinking. We came back together as a class, and I asked each small group what it had discussed, purposefully leaving the question a little vague to solicit a wide range of answers. For example, one group mentioned land exploration and how some explorers, as they searched uncharted territory, would find cultures, animals, and natural formations they did not know existed. Another group looked at exploration from the perspective of medical discoveries.

"You mean it doesn't have to be just about land?" one student asked after this group presented their ideas.

"No," I said. "It can be about anything people explore."

"Can we have some more time?" another student asked. "I have some more ideas."

"Would other groups like more time to think about the question?" I asked, certain that they were ready to move forward with the lesson. To my surprise, every group wanted more time to think about the question.

I happily gave them more time because it was clear they were genuinely engaged in the topic. Colson's group began thinking in terms of space. They wrote questions, ideas, current knowledge, and more on their chart paper. Mya's group discussed technology, wondering if artificial intelligence would one day take over the world. As they delved into their topics, their pieces of chart paper filled up with more and more ideas and questions. Before class ended, I asked them to write one question about exploration that they still had, and we posted them in the classroom. The next day, we started class by exploring those questions on the Internet. Even several weeks after this lesson, we were still answering questions and writing new ones. And, yes, I give them time to answer the questions they generate.

So how might this work in a different content area? What content are you currently teaching that would allow students to think deeply about a topic with a small group of their peers?

Turn and Talk

In our teaching, we often ask students to turn and talk with a table partner. We want to know what students are thinking, how they arrived at their conclusion, and any questions they have. When they discuss a topic or specific concept with another person, students are able to argue, defend, and explain their reasoning, and their original ideas are expanded and enriched.

During turn-and-talk time in language arts, you might have students select a specific novel or short story and:

- Discuss a fictional character who is struggling with a tough decision.

- Imagine how a story would be different if a character's gender were different.

- Put themselves in the character's shoes and discuss whether they would make the same decisions.

- Discuss how your differences might affect the outcome of the story.

During turn-and-talk time in math or science, you might ask students to tackle a problem and:

- Discuss as many different ways you can think of to get to the same solution.

- Change one piece of the equation. How will that affect the outcome?

- Explain how to solve this problem if they aren't allowed to use the word _____?

Ask Questions and Listen

I (Todd) still remember when my friend Eric Sheninger visited my campus one day. Eric is a senior fellow with the International Center for Leadership in Education (ICLE) and an award-winning administrator and author of several education books. As I took him around and showed him different classrooms and shared ideas for the future of our campus, he asked me, "What do the kids think? Have you asked them what they want?"

That question hit me like a ton of bricks. My answer was "no." I hadn't taken the time to sit with our students and ask them what they wanted out of their school. So I formed leadership teams on each grade level comprised of students who were natural leaders and those who hadn't yet realized their potential. I met with the groups every two weeks to do nothing more than to ask them what they wanted out of their school, their classrooms, the lessons their teachers were providing, the playground equipment, and so much more.

Some of their answers veered towards the wildly impossible—build a pool and fill it with Jell-O—but most of the conversations were enlightening. They asked for certain songs to be played on the morning announcements, for the school to purchase more flexible seating, to take time to celebrate teachers who go above and beyond, for the library to order specific books, and for more class pets.

At the end of the year, when I polled the students and asked them what they enjoyed most about being on this committee, my favorite answer was, "I felt like someone at this school was finally listening to me. And more than that, they took some of my ideas and used them. It made me feel like this school and my classroom were really mine too!"

> Ask your students what they think of your learning environment, the activities you plan, and the tests you give.

It is so important for us to take time to ask students for their ideas. They want to be heard, and more than that, they want to know that we, as adults in charge, will actually implement some of their ideas. Ask your students what they think of your learning environment, the activities you plan, and the tests you give. We bet you might be surprised by some of their answers, and you'll find yourself creating a classroom that truly belongs to all of you. We predict the learning will improve as well.

Stories and Healing

The day I (Travis) decided to share my personal writing with my students, I was terrified. I had never taken that step and certainly had never asked for their feedback on a piece of my writing. But I was making important changes in my teaching—renouncing worksheets and the formulaic writing exercises that used to dominate my classes. We were finally studying the craft of writing by analyzing articles, book chapters, poems, and short stories. If my students were to become real writers and readers, they had to emulate the practices of real writers and readers, so I offered up one of my own essays. It was a memoir of sorts, recounting a heartrending and formative experience from my childhood. I didn't make the decision to share the essay lightly. Reaching that point took time, courage, and a recognition that my students and I shared the same fears about writing.

> You own everything that happened to you. Tell your stories.
>
> —Anne Lamott

I knew that conversations about reading and writing were where the real connections were made; however, the dialogue in reading conferences with students unearthed stories of suffering for which there was little to no resolve. They were reading books about controversial topics such as teen pregnancy, drug abuse, physical abuse, and foster care. I would ask them how they related to these books, and they were honest, but they would whisper, afraid that others would hear. Like many teachers, I have students who are dealing with emotional angst, trauma, even probation; for them, these issues are daily battlegrounds. They connected with the books because they saw themselves in the characters, and they could empathize with the pain and anguish often pervasive in young adult literature.

In the midst of their problems, I was still expecting them to attend class and internalize curriculum, a necessity for passing my class and preparing for a future of writing and reading. Internalizing content doesn't really matter, though, when you're facing problems like these kids. Survival was what mattered, and editing a poem or reimagining an opening paragraph in narrative carried little weight. During writing workshop, I noticed limited engagement as they pecked away on their Chromebooks, just fulfilling an assignment, biding time until the class ended. Try as I might, they were unwilling to converse about current events, poems, or even short stories. I was certain that they would find the morbidity of Poe's "Annabel Lee" delightful and Gaiman's opening paragraphs in *The Graveyard Book* lush with imagery. These texts have captivated students of mine for years. With this group, attempts at large-group discussion elicited very little conversation, and when they responded through writing, they wrote superficial sentences, scratching the surface of the narratives. I even asked them to create storyboards and character sketches based on these professional works, but they just weren't interested in drafting something worthwhile. Finally, I realized I was the problem.

> Finally, I realized
> I was the problem.

The writing I was asking them to complete held no value for them, and my class could hardly be considered a workshop environment. I was giving them space and time to write, but I was still trying to control the outcome. They needed a chance to connect with the act of writing. My shortcomings were easily recognizable: I had not given my students a foundation for writing, one that would carry them throughout the year. Writing about literature is a necessary skill, but without the fundamental experience of writing from their own lives, topics about which they were experts, they had no investment in the writing process. They had to start by writing about experiences that held value in their lives. That was the writing that would matter to them.

Although I had not started my workshop in the most engaging way, I believed I could change its course and get them interested in writing. My students are the experts of their pasts, and fusing that expertise with writing would empower them, giving them confidence, showing them that stories unite with readers (see Chapter 9). Personal narratives are powerful, and with the right blend of words, writers can craft passages with vivid imagery. Getting them to write about the hardships they endured would not be an easy task, but Kittle's words about modeling our writing for our kids resonated in my mind as I planned for the next few days of instruction.

I wrote a brief memoir without the intention of sharing it with my students. It was for me, not an audience. But after hearing some of my students' stories and realizing they were troubled, hurting, and angry, I felt I should share it with them.

"Change Can Be Difficult"

A Brief Memoir by Travis Crowder

When I reflect on my past, vivid, colorful memories flood my mind. My parents built a home full of warmth and love. Both of them were hard workers and they instilled in me a drive to achieve greatness. My father bruised his hands from hours of hard labor, and he was willing to sacrifice comfort for the sake of our family. Although rough and calloused from work, his hands were gentle. They wiped away tears, helped me with homework, patted my back before bedtime. Like all children, my vision of the world was not a realistic one; it was clouded by the spirit of love I felt when I was safely ensconced in our house. Home was a haven, a protection from the ugliness of the outside world. At that point in my life, my imagination was not tamed by the terrible reality of our financial situation. In truth, money was almost nonexistent, and my parents struggled to make ends meet; I never understood the hardship because they protected me from it. They cast this protection like it was a charm, but unfortunately, it was short-lived.

By the time I was in eighth grade, I was well aware of the financial burden that had crept over our family. My father worked diligently, but the income was a pittance, never fully providing the funds we needed. On school mornings, he would always ask if I had money for lunch. I often felt guilty for taking money from him because I was beginning to understand the issue with finances. Several times he would give me the last few dollars in his wallet, and even when I refused, worried he would have nothing to buy his lunch with, he forced me to take it.

One morning, I asked him for two dollars for lunch. He opened his wallet, and it was empty except for some receipts. He sighed, and I knew his mind was plagued with worry. "Hang on," he said. He walked to the kitchen cabinet where our family kept a canister with spare change. He pulled it down from the cabinet, twisted off the lid, and brought out four penny rolls. "Will they let you pay with this?" he asked.

"I think so," I said.

"Well if they don't, ask them if you can charge it. I'll pay it as soon as I can," he said, turning away from me. I'm certain he had tears in his eyes.

In the moments leading up to lunch, I began worrying. If I took the penny rolls out of my pocket and if they didn't accept them, I would look like a fool. If they did accept them, and classmates saw me paying with an embarrassing form of payment, I feared I would be ridiculed. Knowing I had charged my lunch in previous weeks, I feared suffering the condescension of the cafeteria cashiers. They were known to be acerbic, and I wasn't sure I could handle their rudeness that day.

To save myself from as much embarrassment as possible, I decided to ask a cashier about the penny rolls before going through the line. If they wouldn't take them, I wouldn't go through the line. I'd just eat when I returned home. I approached the least busy cashier and asked rather quietly, "Can I pay for my lunch with penny rolls?" I assumed she didn't understand how embarrassed I was (it's hard to believe she was just too rude not to care), because she said back, rather loudly, "I don't know if we take penny rolls. You'll have to ask our manager. She's over there!" she said, as she pointed to the front of the cafeteria. The students in the lunch line were looking at me, and I could tell they were amused at the incident. I was dismissed to the cafeteria's overseer, a harsh woman who was anything but pleasant, and as I approached her, I took into account that she was talking to another adult. I waited. I waited some more. She never acknowledged I was standing there, even though I did small things, like moving into her line of sight or clearing my throat to make my presence known.

The lunch line was starting to diminish, and I was still standing there waiting for her to acknowledge me. I was frustrated and embarrassed, and I could see some kids whispering, wondering what I was doing. It fueled my anger and I was ready to burst into tears.

Right before tears slipped from my eyes, one of the kinder cafeteria ladies approached me. "Honey, what do you need?" Her words were comforting, and I was grateful.

"Can I pay for my lunch with penny rolls?" I asked.

"You sure can," she said.

I've never forgotten her soft smile, how she welcomed me into the lunch line, accepted my money, and gave me back my change without question or a sign of ridicule. I've also never forgotten the words of the other cashier, who said, "Guess you can pay with those things," as I walked to my table with my tray of food.

That day I realized the supreme importance of kind words and acceptance. It was the first time I had experienced judgment because of money. I had been protected from such hateful attitudes, but as I ate my lunch, I began to understand the rudeness my parents had to endure. I had enough money to pay for my food, but my method of payment was different. How could paying with change be so difficult? Maya Angelou, one of my favorite poets, said people will forget things about you, but they will never forget how you made them feel. Emotions are fragile things; when they are destroyed, we never forget the people who destroyed them. My attitude toward people changed that day because I saw how rude they can be. I was hurt, and even now, when I remember this part of my past, I cringe at the memory. Sure, I eventually healed, but I have never forgotten.

Change can be difficult.

Having never read any of my work to a class, I was terrified of their reactions. But after sharing my story with them, I noticed an immediate change in the tone of the classroom. They were shocked that I had written something for them, and even questioned the authenticity of my memoir. "It's all real," I assured them. "Now, tell me what you noticed about the structure of my writing."

> **After sharing my story with them, I noticed an immediate change in the tone of the classroom.**

The discussion wasn't perfect, but they could point out the introduction and identify the paragraphs that focused on the central idea of the memoir. And when I asked them to write their own memoir, they didn't hesitate.

We wanted to take the time to share with you a few examples of stories students shared when we were vulnerable in our writing for them to see. Students ranging in age from seven to fifteen blew us away with honesty and passion we had never seen before. Students began writing about heartache, loss, separation, death, and financial struggles that had left indelible marks on their memory.

Faith

Faith, whose defiance had led to several suspensions the year before, wrote beautifully about the death of her grandmother. She explained, "I didn't show my hurt right then because I tried to act strong. When I got home, I burst into tears. I felt like I was now alone, and she was the person I was closest to. I could talk to her about anything. I could trust her, but that day, all of that was gone for good. I said, 'I love you' for the very last time." In her reflection about this piece, Faith said her grandmother's death had been tragic and that writing about it helped get some of the anger and frustration out of her system.

Annie

Annie described the death of her father in ways that made me (Travis) cringe as I read her words. She wrote, "My dad passed away almost two years ago. It was very hard. I wanted to be with him in the ground. I thought there was no purpose in my life." At times while writing, she would start crying, declaring the memoir too difficult to write. She persisted, though, and later reflected that writing the memoir had helped her deal with her father's death.

Robert

Robert was a consistent discipline issue in all of his classes. His disrespect was a challenge for all of his teachers. When he was asked to write about something that broke his heart, his story caught me (Todd) off-guard. He wrote about coming to school that day and being angry because he didn't know any other way to feel. "I can't get those flashing red and blue lights out my mind. When the police pulled my brother over, with me in the front seat, I just knew they were going to arrest him. I watched as he quickly tried to hide the drugs he was going to sell later. My brother, the only one in my family I feel like I can count on, was taken out of his car and handcuffed while I could do nothing but gaze at the floorboard, knowing he was headed back to prison. After the officer brought me to school today, anger is the only thing that feels right." After conferencing about his story, Robert expressed regret that so often he chooses to be angry and defiant towards his teachers. He admitted he doesn't know what to feel because he is overwhelmed with so many emotions. After sharing the story about his brother, Robert's writing took off like never before. "I think I've found a way to feel something again," he said. "I have to write what's in my head down on paper and get it out of me."

"I think I've found a way to
feel something again." he said.
"I have to write what's
in my head down on paper
and get it out of me."

Constance

Constance, a bright and bubbly third-grader, tried but never could get the words on the page to match the words she saw in her mind. She struggled day after day with her dyslexia and other learning impairments but refused to let that bring her down. One day she learned about Google Doc's text-to-speech feature. Sitting in the back corner of the classroom, Constance spoke into her computer, weaving a beautiful story about riding horseback through the fields at her home. "I felt the wind blow through my hair as I rode my horse faster and faster. I wasn't scared. I wasn't tied down. I was free. Free to just feel the wild animal beneath me and take in the beauty of the nature around me. Free from the fear that the words in my head will never be the words I can write on paper. Free to have not a care in the world." Wow! When given the right tools, eight-year-old Constance, who had always been at war with the words in her head, finally told her story.

Your Turn

What story from your past is thumping inside of your heart? Is there a time when you learned a valuable lesson and the learning experience has never left your mind? We challenge you to write this story, and if possible, share it with your students. Give them space and time to write their own. We grow by writing and confronting pieces of our pasts. Share your stories. You own them.

> You'll also be surprised at
> how much you can learn
> from a child when they begin to
> trust you because they see you
> show true pieces of yourself.

You'll also be surprised at how much you can learn from a child when they begin to trust you because they see you show true pieces of yourself. When we write about painful memories, it can be a searing experience that we resist undertaking because we do not want to resurrect the hurt. Our students feel the same way. Yet there is something cathartic about writing. When we spill our emotions onto blank pages, we can see, through words, the problems that plague us. It is a unique way of healing.

If we want our students to write, we will fail miserably until we let them write about the things that are meaningful to them.

As a teacher, it is easy to get lost in curriculum, testing, department meetings, and traditional methods of writing instruction. But if we can get lost in the journey of writing, the rewards are far greater for our students and for us. We believe the best teachers learn alongside their students. They become better writers by writing for and with their students.

Even now, as published authors, we find ourselves insecure about the words we place upon the page. We share those insecurities with our students and also with our staff and colleagues. If we truly want to grow, we have to share the struggles along with the successes and finished pieces.

Difficult Conversations

As educators, it is imperative that we have difficult conversations with our students. Conversations that lead to deeper thinking, challenge our currently beliefs, and force us to explain ourselves. Those moments yield the truest work from our students and help us grow in the process as well.

Honestly, this has been a tough year for many students. Threats of deportation, inhumane displays of racism, caustic rhetoric, and implicit silence—especially from national leaders—have caused a descent into uncertainty and fear. Our children are seeking to be understood while simultaneously seeking to understand. They have questions about current events and the choices that people make. Ambiguity reigns supreme through their eyes, and in school, where they learn about right and wrong, it's no wonder they have a strong sense of justice. They want to see good prevail in the end. But we know that does not always happen. We know they are living in a world where the lines of justice begin to blur depending on a given number of variables.

Teachers are often discouraged from having these difficult conversations with students because it becomes political, and there are strong allegiances to varying ideologies within our communities. But our students are still seeking an understanding of this world in which they live, and we need to provide a safe space for them to discuss their fears, their worries, their uncertainties.

> We need to provide
> a safe space
> for them to discuss
> their fears,
> their worries,
> their uncertainties.

For campus administrators, it is equally important that you have difficult conversations with staff members as well. It's a powerful moment to utilize a faculty meeting or a PLC meeting around a topic that will generate vastly different opinions. That topic might be how to diversify our own learning, or how to deal with a child suffering from abuse, or how to handle adult disagreements in front of students. Whatever the issue, making time for those conversations is a must. When we don't, those problems fester and grow and become something much worse.

Neither of us seeks controversy. In fact, we both despise confrontation and often find ourselves avoiding it at all costs. Our world, however, is replete with controversy, and it is a world our students will inhabit as decisionmakers. We want our classrooms and schools to be a place where ideas are validated, where tough issues are discussed, and where students are able to think through problems with their peers. Adults are never handed worksheets and asked to fill them out before they vote. We listen, read, watch, and extrapolate from evidence; then, we make decisions. That is what we want our students doing. Reading, talking, listening, writing, and making decisions based on those actions. That is what thinkers do.

Navigating Tough Subjects with Books

> One child, one teacher, one book, and one pen can change the world.
>
> —Malala Yousafzai

> A book is a loaded gun in the house next door. Who knows who might be the target of a well-read man?
>
> —Ray Bradbury, Fahrenheit 451

Books are potent things.

We've written that sentence dozens of times, weaving it into blog posts and magazine articles we've been asked to write. We've scribbled it inside almost every notebook we've kept as educators, a small sentence that houses so much truth and understanding. As students have fallen in love with books and have developed reading identities, the sentence has glimmered with new meaning, for us and our students. It is beautiful to behold.

> Arm teachers
> with books.

There is a frightening narrative unfolding at this moment, one that advocates arming teachers in response to the horrific school shootings across the country. We propose a completely different, less violent option: Arm teachers with books. We have witnessed the mesmerizing power that books have over our students. When they read something they love, they want to talk and write about it. They also want to act, to do something in response to the things they read. We have watched students become social justice warriors. Armed with the beautiful ideas from books they read, our students want to seek change in their world, using their reading lives as ammunition. Most recently, one of these students proved it to be true, that a strong reading life is a loaded gun, and with it, we have a chance to change others.

His name is Dane. When he entered the class in late August, you could sense his negative stance toward reading and writing. *I am not inclined to appreciate reading and writing,* he seemed to say with his posture, comments, and the honest answers he provided on his interest inventory. His perspective about language arts, especially a reading and writing workshop, was anything but positive.

In late October, his attitude began to transform. He heard a book talk about *Dear Martin* by Nic Stone, a gripping novel about social justice and the racial disparity that exists in our country. A part of that book was read aloud, and Dane, who usually slouched in his seat during book talks, held onto every word that was read from the book. His interest was piqued. During independent reading time, he asked if he could read the book, stating that he wanted a book where the main character looked like him and understood his experience.

After reading *Dear Martin,* he read *The Hate U Give* by Angie Thomas, *The March Trilogy* by John Lewis, and *When I Was the Greatest* by Jason Reynolds. Reading conferences with him were incisive and pleasant, and by January, he was writing in his notebook about big ideas and themes. Conversations about the author's craft encouraged him to write poems much like Jason Reynolds's poetry. He gleaned inspiration from his writing and ideas, and flipping through his notebook, reading what he had written nudged him further in his writing. "Tell me more," he would see written in the margins, knowing that stories and poems and letters had layers that more writing would unearth. Dane had fallen in love with words and reading. But his attitude and posture on this one day seemed to be telling a completely different story.

During independent reading, his eyes were averted from the page, sharply focused on the blank space in front of him. With his right hand he twisted ringlets of his hair, and with his left hand, he fanned the pages of his book. He was asked if everything was okay? "Yes, sir," he responded. For a moment, his eyes returned to the page, but almost immediately, he resumed the same distant stare, focusing on empty space, his mind anywhere but class.

When independent reading ended, everyone was asked to get their writing notebooks out and turn so they could see the board at the front of the room. Langston Hughes's "I, Too" and Andra Day's "Rise Up" were the pieces of writing that were being focused on for the quick write and discussion before students began using them as ways to see intertextual relationships with their independent reading. Dane turned so he could see the board, but once he saw the poem and song, he smiled and turned back around. No negative attitude had been seen from him in quite some time. Where was the writer, the reader, the poet?

During the quick write, I (Travis) decided to read over shoulders as opposed to writing with my students. I needed to figure out what was going on, confident that Dane's writing would give me a window into his mind. When I looked at his work, I could tell that he was dutifully working in his notebook, but there was no joy. When I approached his group, he did not look up from his notebook, but as I turned to walk away, he said, "Mr. Crowder, can I talk to you after class?"

"Sure," I said. "Is everything okay?"

"Yeah, well, I just need to talk with you about a social justice issue."

"I'll be happy to talk to you," I said.

And he went back to his notebook. For the remainder of class, he worked in his notebook, hardly speaking to the others in his group, intensely focused on the page in front of him. He was writing, but it was with purpose. Glancing over his shoulder as surreptitiously as possible, I noticed him working on Hughes's "I, Too", writing his thoughts and the personal connections he had made around the poem, which he had pasted in his notebook. He was filling the page with vigor and attentiveness, channeling his ideas onto the lines, a mind consumed with something that had precipitated today's class. He loved writing, but today he was on a mission. I was curious and *worried*.

> He was writing.
> but it was with purpose.

Class ended, students packed up their belongings and ushered out of my room. Dane walked to the front of the room and stood in front of me, seemingly searching for the right words. "So, something happened," he said. "I just need to get it off my chest."

"What's up?" I asked, concern, I'm sure, apparent in my voice.

And he told me. He explained how, earlier that morning at breakfast, a fellow seventh grader had approached him and said, "What up, n----!" Repulsed at her language, he asked her to stop, but in reply, she commented that, "Y'all people say it all the time, so why can't I say it?" His attempts at explaining appropriate language were insufficient. Out of spite, she began saying it just to seek retaliation, wanting him to become angered. "But I didn't," he said. "I wanted to be the bigger person."

As the day went on, his thinking sought the memory of the incident, dragging it to the forefront of his mind. By the time he reached language arts and he saw that we were reading a poem by Langston Hughes, the experience from earlier that day was burdensome. And so he wanted to talk to me, the person who had suggested he read *Dear Martin*, the book that ignited his reading life. "I knew you'd understand," he said.

"I don't know what to do," Dane continued. "Maybe I just needed to get it off my chest." He started to leave, but I stopped him.

"Dane, do you remember what Justyce did?"

He smiled at me, recognizing the main character from *Dear Martin*. "Yeah."

"Do you think that would help?"

"Are you telling me I need to write to Dr. Martin Luther King, Jr.?"

"I'm not telling you to do anything, Dane. But do you think writing to Martin Luther King, Jr., or Rosa Parks, or Malcolm X, or John Lewis would help?"

He smiled at me and nodded. "I know what I want to tell him. Thanks, Mr. C. Can I have a note to my next class?"

I wrote him a note and watched him leave my room. The following morning, he brought me the letter he had penned, written with conviction to MLK, Jr. There was a rich authenticity to his letter: There was a significant audience, as well as a beautiful purpose. "I showed it to my mom this morning, Mr. C. She sat down at the kitchen table and cried." When he walked away, so did I.

He wrote:

Dear Martin,

I really do not know how to start, so I'm going to just jump right into it.

So it's Black History Month, and I'm being really cautious. Some, not all, but some people are saying mean things. I feel like people are running over us. Well, not all people, but some. I want to put an end to this.

I wanna protest. Not sure if I can, but I really want to.

OK, so there was this girl who used the "N" word when she spoke to me this morning. I was so mad because then other people started using it. I felt like it got out of hand. I'm still angry. I really don't know what to do. I just felt like I should come to you. I want to speak out. I want to say something, but I don't want to say something that will hurt someone. Or get me in trouble.

Maybe this will help.

Thank you so much,

Dane

Since writing his first letter to MLK, Jr., Dane's writing has found a courage and intensity that it did not have before. He has written more letters to MLK, Jr., and they have become deeply honest, probing at issues he is trying his best to understand and overcome. But more importantly,

Dane connected with a book and used it to leverage his feelings, ideas, and reactions. This is a social justice move, a civic action that all students need to participate in, and students like Dane are leading the way.

In a time when politicians and other leaders are advocating for arming teachers with guns, we are advocating for a completely different way to arm us. Give us books, ones that will change our students' lives, give them a renewed purpose, and encourage them to crusade for change within their country and world. When students like Dane are moved by books and use them as sources of strength and resilience, we are emboldened by their noble act. Books are powerful things. And they change us.

> Books are potent, and with them,
> we can arm our students.

Arm us with books, with gorgeous, riveting prose that will engage students in reading and civic action. Arm us with books, with lyrical poetry, inspiring imagery, and explorations of the human condition that expose all that is good, evil, and noble in this world. Books are potent, and with them, we can arm our students. Dane could have chosen a different strategy to deal with his anger, but he chose to use Nic Stone's novel as a guide, as a mentor. A solitary book changed him and gave him a way to rise above the ignorance. We want this for all our students.

Arm us with books. Because the pen is mightier than the sword.

And books will change hearts and minds.

Navigating Tough Subjects through Images

Using photography is a great way to frame thinking, both in language arts and social studies. When you ask your students to look at a photograph and write what they see, what they are thinking, and any questions they might have, they are often able to gain a new perspective. Taking the time to display photographs on the board at the front of the classroom is also important; other times, students can complete a gallery walk and respond to the photographs affixed to pieces of chart paper.

Starting the school year with a big question is a great idea: What is a community, and how is it created? You can have students divide into small groups to ponder this question and give them a chance to share their thinking with the entire class. This exercise allows you to hear your students' viewpoints and allows them to consider their own rationale.

Next, move to silent conversations. In the middle of large pieces of chart paper, you can tape photographs that encourage students to think about community, ask questions, and consider the people responsible. The image above is one of refugees. Heated debates have risen in the political realm, mostly based on ignorant rhetoric, but it is impossible to deny the humanity and suffering evident in this photograph. Understanding this big question would involve speaking to the hearts of your students.

Pencil in hand, each student can meander around the classroom, looking at the photographs and adding their thinking on the chart paper. You can ask them to:

- Jot down questions they have about the photograph.
- Identify emotions they notice.
- Write down what it reminds them of.
- Reference a book that it could be similar to.
- Write what is going through their minds as they look at the photograph.
- Respond to at least five or more classmates by answering questions, posing additional questions or extending someone else's idea.

Students should be encouraged to comment with sensitivity, particularly when the photographs depict intense situations. When this was completed, students were incredibly well-behaved during this silent conversation, focusing on the images, responding, and commenting on the responses of their classmates.

Once finished, you can ask them to share their thinking with their group. You might hear questions like these:

- "Did you see the picture of the flooding? Why wasn't anyone helping those people?"
- "Is there a way America can help?"
- "What's so difficult about helping someone find a home?"
- "What if that happened to us?"
- "Who took the pictures? Couldn't they have helped?"

A young person's sense of justice might be awakened during this exercise, and we guarantee you'll love hearing their questions.

> Everything in your classroom
> should eventually lead
> to writing.

Everything in your classroom should eventually lead to writing. Give your students time to write personal responses to the photographs, using your big question about community as a starting point. Encourage them to think about who is responsible for what they're seeing. Encourage them to see humanity.

Your Turn

We want you to consider your own content areas. What tough issues, perhaps controversial ones, could students talk about in your content area and know it was a beautifully safe space? How might you lead students into a discussion about world hunger, disease, poverty, abuse, and destruction? Could you provide data for students to view and extrapolate information from? Could students write the narrative represented in sets of numbers related to a tough issue? Could students write to entities or individuals to express concern about an issue? Don't be afraid to step outside and try something different to bring about your students' humanity into your subject area.

Alternative Viewpoints

We also find it incredibly important that, if you're going to have critical conversations with your students (or with other adults for that matter), you do not create a vacuum of resources. Students and adults need to be privy to information from all sides and especially information that they may not necessarily agree with.

We have seen, time and time again, how quickly someone can become closed-minded to new ideas or solutions when they choose to only consume information from one source or information that they agree with.

I (Todd) still remember when I first heard about the book *For White Folks Who Teach in the Hood . . . And the Rest of Y'all Too* by Christopher Emdin. I was intrigued by the title alone and wanted to read more. You see, as a white male educator, I know there are certain privileges that have been afforded to me. And certain preconceived notions that I carry. I have worked tirelessly the last few years of my career educating myself on the struggles, history, and success of others who do not look or sound like me. As I read the book, my mind was blown time and time again with information and revelations. Of how simply something I can do or say can be misunderstood or the amount of misunderstanding I was doing with my students!

Whether it's books about LGBTQ, Muslim, or minority characters, or so many others, it doesn't matter. I can't even begin to tell you how much I have grown as an individual. I can't consume the stories fast enough. Granted, I may not agree with everything that I read, but every time I pick up a book, starring a character who looks or sounds nothing like me, I leave that story having learned something. It has taught me more empathy for others than anything else I have ever done.

When we bring all sorts of articles and opinions to the table, we can then learn how to have respectful conversations. We can learn that we don't have to agree with someone to respect their rights to a differing opinion. And if we can create more citizens like that, think of how much better our world would be.

> When we bring all sorts of articles and opinions to the table, we can then learn how to have respectful conversations.

The same is true of the adults we work with. Administrators need to take time to bring conflicting research to the table and have teachers dissect and discuss it. To continue to have the conversation that there isn't one perfect way to teach. To grow our libraries and our horizons by introducing staff to books and articles with diverse characters from all walks of life, even those we don't agree with. Because the moment you don't have those conversations, that's the moment you silence someone's voice.

If We . . .

If we want students to read more, they need to talk about the books they are reading with their peers.

If we want students to write more, we need to give them opportunities to talk with their peers about their writing.

If we want students to think more, we have to give them opportunities to talk about their thinking with their peers.

If we want students to develop an appreciation of our content, we have to give them time to develop that appreciation by talking about it with their peers.

If we want students to think about the world in terms of science and appreciate the metaphors of scientific language, we have to give them a chance to talk about it.

If we want students to see the logic and rhythm of the world through numbers and sequence, we have to give them opportunities to talk about how that logic and rhythm exist in our world.

If we want students to excel, we have to provide opportunities for dialogue within our classroom.

THINGS TO THINK ABOUT AND TWEET

What critical conversations have you recently had with students?

What critical conversations have you had with your colleagues or administrators?

Why do you think it is important to share alternative viewpoints?

#SparksInTheDark

If there is no struggle, there can be no progress.

—Frederick Douglass

Chapter 8

Challenge Them

EDUCATORS HEAR A GREAT deal about the importance of challenging students with more rigor, depth, and complexity. It's a daunting task. Not only must educators continually learn new ways to sharpen our students' thinking; they have to deal with students who push back when they find themselves in challenging environments. But just because something is difficult doesn't mean it isn't worth doing.

When I (Todd) altered my classroom instruction from a lecture-and-worksheet model to a flipped project-based model, I was elated to try something that was new and much more my style. A style that allowed for more talk, creativity, and growth than ever before. I just knew my students were going to love it too. I mean, come on, lectures and worksheets are the worst! My new approach was going to be way more exciting.

It didn't exactly start off that way. Instead of rave reviews, I got immediate pushback from students—and a few parents. All of my carefully crafted exercises and thought-provoking activities were met with major resistance. Why? According to many of the students, class had become too difficult. It wasn't so difficult that they were unable to actually complete the work, but it was harder than they had ever worked before, and they were not amused. They weren't used to it. I can't tell you how times I heard, "Can't you just give a worksheet to do? That's so much easier." I was floored. Who asks for worksheets?

But those are the kinds of students we had created as a school. They had been spoon-fed information and expectations, and they hadn't had to truly tax their brains. But where was the real learning in answering a few multiple-choice questions? How was that ever going to produce lifelong learners?

I share this because I want you to know that, when you challenge your students and present them with activities that depart from the norm, there will be some grumbling. But do your best to stick with it. I did, and during my final two years in the classroom, I was able to provide far more profound and rigorous learning opportunities.

Challenging Readers and Writers

Sometimes as educators, we spend a large chunk of our planning and instruction on reaching the struggling children. What if, instead, we focused on challenging all students? What if we set the standard high and worked to raise every student to their own individual success level?

It's possible, but we have to be willing to do the hard work. We have to challenge our readers and writers. If we don't, we will end up with students who only work to complete an assignment to please a teacher. They won't grow into adults who are looking to continually push the boundaries of what they're truly capable of reading and writing.

Until several years ago, I (Travis) believed the classroom environment I had created for my students was supportive of rigorous learning. Desks were in rows, students took notes while I lectured, and assignments consisted of worksheets and projects. We tackled challenging material—*A Midsummer Night's Dream* by William Shakespeare, "The Lottery" by Shirley Jackson, "The Cask of Amontillado" by Edgar Allan Poe, and poems by Robert Frost, Emily Dickinson, and William Cullen Bryant, as well as multiple legends and myths. I also spent quite a few weeks teaching grammar principles and sentence structure. Students would talk about how difficult my class was and how challenged they were, but they did not love it. They were merely observing reading and writing, never experiencing them. I finally decided to make a change, and in the course of a year, I shifted my classroom from a traditional environment to a workshop classroom.

That shift resulted in much more student choice in both reading, writing, and social studies—and an overall project-based approach to teaching—it also changed the physical characteristics of my classroom. To encourage collaboration and accommodate the turn-and-talk activities, I disassembled my neat little rows and rearranged the desks into groups of four, brought in comfier chairs, and stocked my bookshelves with library books I knew my students would want to read.

In the end, this challenged them more than my previous method of teaching.

Here's how.

First, reading itself is a complex process. When students encounter a text independently, they are responsible for making sense of the words, the sentences, the figurative language, and, in the end, the meaning. If driven by choice, students will choose increasingly more difficult books. I often hear the argument that free-choice, independent reading does not promote a rigorous classroom because students will select simplistic novels instead of challenging ones. I disagree. When presented with choices, students will seek more rigorous reading. Finishing a book boosts confidence and only encourages them to read more. Choice matters, and it is a key to moving students to more rigorous reading.

Second, students are given a space to read, write, and share. Each day they are with a group, inches away from someone who could provide them with reading suggestions, writing feedback, and writing ideas. I guide them with questions that encourage in-depth conversations. Some of these questions are:

- What are you reading? What made you select it?
- Would someone in your group enjoy this book? Your teacher? Why?
- How does this piece of writing teach us a lesson about life?
- How do life lessons help us think about literature?
- Look back through your writing notebook. What is a piece of writing you wish to grow? How can you grow it? (I ask this question often.)
- How is the book you are reading structured?
- How can you change this piece of writing so that it is easier for a reader to navigate?
- When you read this book, where do you see yourself in the story?
- Donald Murray says that problems make good subjects. What problem was the author exploring in this novel? What problem are you exploring in your piece of writing?
- What about this book drew you in and made you want to read it? How can you take some of those qualities and incorporate them into your writing?

> We have to persevere and challenge the status quo even when it seems like all we're doing is banging our head against the wall.

Writing is difficult. Being told to "just write" is daunting for a child who is sitting in front of a blank notebook or digital document, searching her mind for the words to begin. I mention this because another way I challenge my students is asking them to take things to full draft as often as possible. Students write in their notebooks often, but they are required to choose two pieces each nine weeks—one short, one longer—to final-ize and submit as part of their grade for my class. To do this, students must have a storehouse of writing from which to choose. They go back through their notebooks and choose the pieces that speak to them, and we spend time writing, conferencing, rewriting, and getting it to a stop-ping place. In the beginning, students struggled with that structure, but as the year continued, I noticed increased confidence in my writers.

Asking deep, thought-provoking questions, altering the learning environment, expecting students to rise to the task given to them; those are what we must have in place in our reading and writing classrooms if we expect to challenge our students. We have to persevere and challenge the status quo even when it seems like all we're doing is banging our head against the wall. Our children might not ask us to challenge them, but they need us to.

Rigorous Reading

Teri Lesesne, *Reading Ladders* revolutionized the way we view inde-pendent reading and skills acquisition in our adolescent readers. Not all students are prepared to read dense, complex literature, but with the right support and a voluminous reading life, they can break through the barriers that have held them hostage as readers. They can read more chal-lenging books, but it takes a reading ladder to get them there.

According to Lesesne, a reading ladder is "a series or set of books that are related in some way . . . and that demonstrate a slow, gradual devel-opment from simple to more complex." A ladder is used as a metaphor for a reading life throughout the text. Readers move up the rungs of the ladder as their reading lives become richer and more complex as a result of more rigorous reading. We often see students who come into our classrooms with experience on only one or two rungs of a metaphorical ladder. When presented with a challenging text, one that is several rungs above their current reading ability, students struggle, sometimes meet-ing us with resistance. An understanding of reading ladders can alter that experience for teachers and students.

Take this to heart: There is plenty of great young adult literature published every year for students to have access to interesting titles, text complexity, and themes that will engage and sustain their attention. More importantly, when students have built a foundation of reading and can move to increasingly more challenging texts, they can move from where they are to the places we would like for them to be as readers.

All Quiet on the Western Front by Erich Maria Remarque is a classic text used in many secondary classrooms. English and history classes read this novel. Although there are different schools of thinking about whole-class novels, we want to discuss how students can build a reading ladder to that text. Since the book focuses on World War I, we will explore texts that are as closely related as possible to that topic.

The first rung of the ladder could be *Megiddo's Shadow* by Arthur Slade. This novel follows Edward, a young man who enlists in World War I after both of his older brothers are killed during combat. There are thought-provoking moments and sections for students to respond to in their notebooks, as well as encourage them to further reading.

A little more challenging could be *Crossing Stones* by Helen Frost, a book of World War I that focuses on two resilient families. This book is also written in verse, which offers its own unique challenge to many readers.

Next, students may want to move to *The Foreshadowing* by Marcus Sedgwick, a novel that follows Sasha, an adolescent who is blessed with foresight. No one will believe her as she tries to explain the horrors that await her brothers in the Great War, but she continues to share the stories and horror that she is "seeing." Themes and vocabulary make this book a bit more rigorous.

As students build their stamina, access more rigorous texts, and read sentences and words that are more challenging, they will create a reading ladder that will take them to *All Quiet on the Western Front*. And this approach works with all texts. *1984. Romeo and Juliet. To Kill a Mockingbird. Hamlet.* Giving students access and choice to books that will transform their reading habits and reading levels is critical.

How Choice Creates Challenge

Choice begets challenge. When students have opportunities to select their own reading material, they may start with something simple. Struggling or inept readers need that foundation. As their confidence in their reading abilities grows, their reading selections will mirror the growth in their reading lives. In other words, students will choose more challenging books.

Reading inventories, given on the first day of school, give me a starting place. I am forever looking for the story: where are students in their reading lives, what conflicts have they encountered, and how I can help them overcome those unresolved obstacles or encourage them to read more challenging books. Some of the questions I ask them include:

- How do you define "good readers?"
- How would you describe your personal reading lives?
- What books have you read and loved?
- What authors are you familiar with?

These questions serve as a foundation to the reading inventory I provide to students on day one of the school year. I use their responses as a guide, choosing books for book talks based on their interests and previous reading habits. Some readers must start with easier reads, but given space and time to read those books, students will grow as thinkers and seek more challenging reading material.

> Some readers must start with easier reads,
> but given space and time to read those
> books, students will grow as thinkers and
> seek more challenging reading material.

Giving students choices in their reading lives does not mean that we are abandoning rigorous literary study. It simply means we are willing to redefine what rigorous study looks like in our classrooms. When students choose, they work harder. They select tasks (in this case, books) that will push them. Don't believe me? I challenge you to try it and watch as students' reading lives explode and their thinking deepens.

Challenge the Adults, Too

We must also challenge the adults with whom we work. We've said it before and we'll say it again—how can we ask our students to show up day after day and learn if we aren't learning ourselves? And not just learning the easy stuff or things we agree with right away or even things that are always at the top of our personal priorities.

I (Todd) love doing staff book studies with my team. We've done this in several ways through the years. Some of the books we've read as an entire team have been *Disrupting Thinking* by Robert Probst and Kylene Beers, *The Book Whisperer* by Donalyn Miller, *Crash Course* by Kim Bearden, and *The Energy Bus* by John Gordon. As we read through the book, we would meet once a week for fifteen minutes and share different things we were learning from the book. But it was more than just trading information. At every meeting, I tried to prepare thought-provoking questions or comments to discuss. My goal was push their thinking and challenge their preconceptions by raising ideas I knew my staff wouldn't always agree with. After all, if we can't have honest and difficult conversations while we're together in a group of our peers, how are we supposed to feel comfortable having those conversations outside of that environment? I wanted to create a school environment in which teachers felt comfortable questioning each other's practices. Not in a negative or judgmental way, but in a professional manner that conveys you're seeking to understand another person's position.

I especially enjoyed the year we gave the staff six different books to choose from, and they formed book clubs and met every other week to talk and share about the book they were reading. Some met in person, others via Voxer, and some shared their ideas in a Google Docs document. They took ownership of their learning and explored their books in the ways they found most convenient and comfortable. And although I am extremely selective when choosing books for our staff to read, they seemed to enjoy having several choices and being able to explore a book I hadn't preselected for everyone.

As educators, we must continually challenge each other. And, teachers, you don't have to wait for your administrator to start a book club on campus. Just do it! Find a book with an engaging topic and invite your colleagues to join you. Even getting three to four other educators together to talk and trade ideas can bring about great change.

And for those of you who are thinking, "I can't even find one other educator who will read a book with me on my campus," never fear. That's why we always preach the power of social media. Every day on Twitter, you will find amazing conversations about pedagogical books—especially works from Dave Burgess Publishing—and many other boundary-pushing topics. It just takes a little courage, so be brave enough to put yourself out there and I know you will reap the rewards.

THINGS TO THINK ABOUT AND TWEET

In what ways can you differentiate your instruction to challenge all of your students at their individual levels?

What challenging text or poem can you use in your instruction to push thinking?

In what ways are you challenging yourself as a reader and a writer?

#SparksInTheDark

Never a day
without a line.

—Anonymous

Chapter 9

Living a Writerly Life

Every Thanksgiving, my (Travis) family takes a trip to Gatlinburg, TN. The frosty mountain town is bursting with energy during this time of year, and the shops that line the main street are alive with festive decorations. Smells of caramel, peppermint, and fudge waft through the air, and as twilight begins, the chilly air begins to sparkle in the lamplight. This quaint place radiates with its own special charm.

My writing muscles are always inspired by the sights, smells, and sounds of Gatlinburg. This past November, I decided to take my laptop to the local Starbucks and return some emails. Linda Rief, teacher, writer, and mentor, had sent me an email about the most recent NCTE conference, and I was anxious to reply. I turned on my computer and tried to connect to the Wi-Fi in Starbucks, but the prodigious number of people in the coffee shop had jammed the Wi-Fi connection, and my computer would not load my most recent emails. So, I walked down the street to the local McDonald's and connected to the Wi-Fi there.

I emailed Linda, spending a line or two lamenting the poor Internet at Starbucks then began working through pieces of the book you now hold in your hands. She emailed back within the half hour. Her email was cordial and delightful (they always are), but at the end, she gave me some of the best writing advice I have ever received: "Put that computer away and get out your writing notebook. Write about the differences between the two places. What do you hear? What do you see?" I chuckled but followed her advice. And I am glad I did!

When we write, we *have* to notice, and we notice by listening and watching. Writing exists in moments that we consider ordinary, but as I often say, there is significance in the ordinary. There were distinct sounds that translated beautifully into poetry. I share this story with my students because I want them to see how writing transcends our perceptions. Student writers often feel that they have nothing to say, nothing to contribute, nothing to explain. But they do.

Writing exists everywhere. We just have to show them where to look.

In *The Art of Teaching Writing*, Lucy Calkins mentions the importance of living a writerly life, of noticing, and using the things we notice as guides in our writing. She says, "Writing allows us to turn the chaos into something beautiful, to frame selected moments, to uncover and celebrate the organizing patterns of our existence." Writers learn to pay attention, find significance in the ordinary, and create beauty from the chaos. Dew drops on flower petals at dusk. Amorphous clouds illuminated by silver strands of light. Blades of grass breaking through the cracks of a sidewalk. The contrast of red mud on a pristine, white floor. Writers see these as more than just observational points. They are moments of reaction, of description, of story.

For my (Travis) entire life, my father has worked as a plumbing contractor, braving the intense heat and numbing cold to provide for our family. When I was young, Dad expected me to work alongside him during breaks from school, mainly winter and summer break, hoping I would learn the family trade. (His father was a plumbing contractor, too.) My early teens are filled with hilarious stories of my poor attempts at gluing pipe together, searching for the cause of a waterline break, or pulling up a commode that was not entirely empty of its contents. In the midst of all the mishaps, there were moments of success, especially when my father stood beside me and guided the process.

> Writing exists everywhere.
> We just have to show them
> where to look.

The biggest successes came from seeing a final product, such as how a perfectly fitted pipe should look when joined with a T-fitting. I inundated my father with questions, uncertain of my ability and fearful that I would detach the wrong fitting or, worse, break something. His patience was golden during this time, and though he did get frustrated with my inadequacy, he was always willing to answer my questions, show me how the finished product should look, and guide my small, trembling hands. Daily practice would have made me a pro. Unfortunately, I was not interested in the art of plumbing and chose to follow my passion as a reader, writer, and thinker. But my father's guidance has translated beautifully to my understanding of student writers and the conditions necessary to help develop their writing abilities.

A Writer's Notebook

Three years ago, I (Travis) discovered Penny Kittle's *Write Beside Them*, which is a must-have for educators who want to make a difference in the writing lives of students. The book resonated with me strongly, and I found myself highlighting passages, writing in the margins, copying excerpts into my personal notebook, and reflecting on certain pieces with fellow teachers and my administrator.

Kittle's words are powerful, and they send a clear message to teachers: Students will write if you guide them through the process. At the end of the book, she leaves teachers with a call to action: Get a notebook and start writing. Writing teachers are writers. There is no way around this statement. If you want to influence the writing lives of your students, you must write. That is where a writing notebook becomes essential. A writing notebook is the perfect place to house your thinking, collect bits of poetry that are meaningful to you, paste newspaper clippings, write sentences from novels that have moved you, staple letters and emails that have touched your heart, and participate in the writing process you expect from your students.

We challenge you to find a notebook, either tangible or digital, and start logging your thinking. Our preference is typically a physical notebook because there is something significant about putting pen to paper. This might not be your style, though. The point is to start writing. Start thinking. And lead your students to deeper, more sophisticated writing through the ideas they compile in their writing notebooks.

We have asked students to keep journals before, requiring that they use a notebook to house their thinking. But our expectations today are much different because we are different teachers—growing and perfecting our craft as time goes by. In *A Writer's Notebook: Unlocking the Writer Within You*, Ralph Fletcher described a writing notebook as a place where "writers react" and where "writers record those reactions." That's what we expect students to do now—to notice what's happening around them, react to it, and chronicle what they're thinking and feeling.

Writers need good things to think about, though. As instructors, it is our job to curate exemplary pieces of writing from a wide range of sources—professionals, other students, and ourselves. If we want them to react, we have to show them how writers react. In *Write Beside Them*, Kittle explains her method of opening her notebook, placing it beneath her document camera, and writing with her students. The very idea horrified both of us at first, thinking that our sacred notebook and writing would be displayed for general viewing, like a patient upon an operating table. But her method was brilliant and worked like a charm. Students need to see the nuts and bolts of the writing process. This is part of the guide's job: showing more than telling.

> This is part of the guide's job:
> showing more than telling.

It's also important to ask students what they notice about a piece of writing. That question provides more insight and showcases student ability more than any comprehension question we could possibly devise. It's a great question to help students react in their writing notebooks. One of our favorite passages is the opening section of *The Notorious Benedict Arnold* by Steve Sheinkin. There is so much imagery, description, and beautiful word choice for students to notice, discuss, and emulate in their own writing. Sharing this piece is perfect for demonstrating description and how an author can weave sentences into a captivating scene. You can also follow Linda Rief's guidelines for an effective quick write, throwing out questions like these:

- What sentences stood out to you?
- What words caught your attention?
- Why did you notice them?
- What about them captivated your attention?

And don't forget to show your students your own reactions to this piece of writing, displayed in your own notebook for all to see.

Helping students develop a writerly life takes time, patience, and guidance. We are both still learning how to do it as we continue down this path. But the one thing we know from experience is without daily writing, without a commitment to a writing life, our students' writing will suffer, and so will our teaching of it.

During my (Travis) first year of teaching, I wanted my students to craft an essay, one with voice and passion. I gently narrowed their topics, offering many choices and giving them one week to craft an essay.

During this week, they were diligent, shoulders hunched over keyboards and eyes fervently scanning articles online. From a distance, it looked academic. At the end of the week, they submitted their final essays, and I was dismayed by the pieces of writing I held in my hands. Their final products were lifeless, lacking voice and passion, and were devoid of any original ideas. This was what they had created after a whole week of thinking, researching, and writing? Something was not right.

But the more I thought about it, I realized that given the writing environment I had created, my students' work was spot on.

The problem was my ignorance. The essays my students wrote were a product of the conditions I had provided. I had given them no texts to model, and as a group, we had not discussed the craft of writing, how authors fuse ideas together into sentences and select specific words to express their thinking. Looking back, I am ashamed of that approach, and today, as a more reflective teacher, I look for articles, poems, paragraphs, book chapters, and sentences that will help my students deepen their awareness of their own writing and help them write beautifully.

It takes practice, though.

One or two poem studies before a major writing project will not elicit the type of writing we want from students. When we transitioned our classrooms from a traditional environment to a workshop enclave, we had and still have plenty of learning to do about what students need to become better writers. The study of writing, built from carefully constructed mentor texts, is an ongoing process. It must be a consistent— we suggest daily—routine. Those living a writerly life are surrounded by good, great, and superlative writing, and we must surround our students with the same if we want them to learn to write with eloquence and conviction.

The Power of Poetry

Poetry is one of the most valued genres of writing in my (Travis) classroom. I use poetry almost daily, exposing my students to poems I believe will fill their minds with wondrous thoughts, tug at their heartstrings, and stimulate their writerly minds. Poems by Billy Collins, Jacqueline Woodson, Kwame Alexander, Pablo Neruda, Maya Angelou, William Stafford, Cynthia Rylant, and Allan Wolf, along with innumerable others, form this corpus of work. And sharing it has reaffirmed my belief that poetry pushes the mind of a writer past the ostensible.

In this section, we will to take you on a journey into classrooms beyond language arts, where students are studying the craft of writing and their work is blossoming into genuine and unique self-expression.

Writing beyond the English/Language Arts Classroom

My (Travis) fellow teacher, Brian Weisend, is such a cool guy. Charismatic and witty, he commands his classroom with a sense of ease, and his kids adore him. Though he is a science teacher, we discuss the art of teaching often, finding the places where language arts and science intersect. There are many. We are both aficionados of big questions, the kind we can pose to our students and give them an entire class period or longer to discuss, research, and write about. We love watching students conduct mini-research assignments, discovering questions of their own and positing theories inspired by our big questions.

Recently, Brian and I were discussing how poetry can be a cool introduction to a lesson. As a science teacher, Brian is used to teaching vocabulary to his students first, a traditional way to introduce scientific concepts and ideas.

"I want to do something different," he told me.

"Like what?" I prompted, knowing that conversation is the basis for many major pedagogical changes.

"Get them talking and writing," Brian said.

"I think I can help," I answered with a smile.

Brian's idea was refreshing. A desire to get students writing in the science classroom was not something I heard often. But Brian was willing to step out of his comfort zone and invite students to read an original poem of his creation, respond to it through discussion, and ultimately craft their own.

Here's the poem:

"Roller Coaster"
By Brian Weisend

I sat idly waiting for them to join me
A jolt, a rush, a climb to feel so free
Those looking for something fun to do
I simply needed a minute or two

Many found their way to me, to check me off their list
I could smell the fear escaping, a gasp and a clenched fist
They joined me one by one
I held them ever so tightly, then reminded them I'll soon
be done

I brought them to the highest point, to look all-around
We waited for but a minute before I dropped them to
the ground
I could hear them breathe, some screamed for
their friend
Hard to avoid the adrenaline that waited at every bend

Their feet dangling so I went faster than before
Kicking, screaming, leaning, all knocking at death's door
Their life turned upside-down, I turned to see their tears
It was at that moment they all realized they'd come to
face their fears

Brian's poem engaged his students in conversation, critical thinking, and writing. Their conversations led them to create their own poems about motion, and throughout the unit of study, students were encouraged to think about poems that could be written about topics they discussed.

Mystery Poems

Not long ago, I (Travis) was in the back room of my apartment, rummaging through boxes and crates, digging through old notebooks, visiting the written history of my past. In one box, a yellow highlighter peeked out from beneath several stacks of papers. My mind often thinks in lines of poetry, and the line, "I glide across sentences, leaving a path of illumination," popped into my mind. I thought about sharing that sentence with my students and asking them to determine the subject I was writing about. Would they be able to? Or what if I turn this line into a full poem and asked them to determine the subject? Could they then write their own?

People who know me chuckle at the messes I can leave behind in rooms I visit. That day I left everything in a giant pile on the floor, notebooks lying open, boxes everywhere, and started writing in my notebook. Two mystery poems came to be.

Interestingly enough, I did not write about a yellow highlighter. I typed the poems and added them to my Google Classroom page, leaving them for students to read, decipher, and use as models to craft their own. You can make them as tricky as you want, but the goal is to obscure the subject of the poem—just a little—and leave clues throughout that will help readers figure it out. Here are the two I wrote:

"Mystery Poem #1"

Weightless and bright,
I sparkle in the light.
Floating,
Graceful,
And a beautiful sight.
You love me as a child,
But fear me when you travel.
Days with me
Might drive a sane person
Wild.
(answer: snow)

"Mystery Poem #2"

I warm your soul,
And taste delightful.
You hold me close
As you inhale the mist
That rises.
I might be a good friend,
But when it's cold
I disappear
Quickly.
"Hershey" might be a good name
For me.
(answer: hot chocolate)

My students love these mystery poems. Poetry is a wonderful place to start when engaging students in conversation, writing, and critical thinking about a lesson or an idea. Consider your subject area and how mystery poems might be used. Get your notebook out, try your hand at a mystery poem, and share it with your students! Do not be afraid of poetry. It is a subtly delightful friend.

Heart Maps

We constantly tell our students good writing comes from deep inside. We want them to write about meaningful things, about experiences that have shaped them as human beings. More than anything, we want them to write about the things they love. Mem Fox, in the article "Notes from the Battleground," discussed the importance of writers "aching with caring about what they write." To ache with caring is to experience concern, heartfelt concern, about the words on the page, the way they are arranged, semantics, word choice, and tone. It also means working with a piece until it says exactly what you want it to or getting it to a point where we can abandon it. That is the kind of writing we want from our students. Many writers, however, need a visual. They need to explore and write about the things that matter to them. In our teaching careers, we have found the best way to get students to explore the things that live in their hearts, things that are worth writing about, is for them to create heart maps.

> They need to explore
> and write about the things
> that matter to them.

One of our favorite professional books is *Awakening the Heart* by Georgia Heard. To get her students writing, Heard told them about how she, a professional poet, used memories from her childhood, people she had met, and things that resided deep in her heart. Students were sent to their seats to write, and when she ambled around her classroom, glancing at the writing her students had produced, she did not see examples of heartfelt poetry. So, she decided to use heart maps.

When we use heart maps with students, we usually ask students to draw a large heart that will take up an entire page in their writing notebooks. Using Georgia Heard's questions as a guide, students are encouraged to include:

- Things they love
- People they love
- Objects that hold memories
- Words people have said to them to inspire them
- Happy and sad memories
- Experiences that live in their hearts, ones that have (possibly) changed them

After students have created the first draft of their heart maps, it's great to let them rest overnight. The following day, and even throughout the year, we find ourselves returning to our heart maps and adding things we realize are missing. From these heart maps, students have people, objects, words, and memories they can write about. It's a superb starting point.

Heart maps can exist outside of language arts and social studies classes. Brian Weisend, the science teacher who used poetry to help teach the concept of motion, has used them with his students. To connect with his students on a personal level, he spent several class periods letting them work on heart maps. He changed the assignment just a bit, though. For his students' heart maps, he asked them to focus on the music that lived in their hearts, crafting his own heart map for students to use as a mentor text.

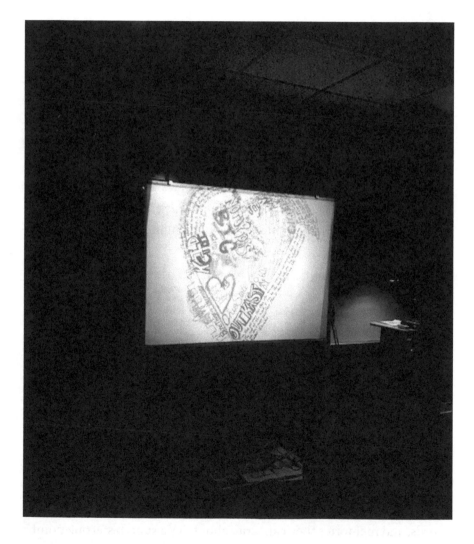

Students loved working on these heart maps in Brian's class, and in the end, they learned something about their teacher and classmates. Heart maps have the power to connect us, showing us the threads that unite us as people.

If you are interested in getting your students to write with conviction and from a place deep inside, Georgia Heard's writings will be an important addition to your storehouse of resources.

Abandoning the Norm

In the afternoons, I (Travis) work with a class of gifted students, helping them develop their craft as writers. This time is set aside as an enrichment period. I want it to be worthwhile. I use quite a few mentor texts to guide their thinking, especially when we start talking about and writing poetry. All writers need models of writing to help them begin crafting their own pieces, but poetry often frightens young writers. Many students come into my class threatened by poetry, thinking they are seeking some deep, hidden message. I want them to unpack a poem as readers and as writers.

One afternoon, during my enrichment class, I decided to use a mentor text from *Immersed in Verse: An Informative, Slightly Irreverent, & Totally Tremendous Guide to Living the Poet's Life* by the amazing Allan Wolf. I use this book often in my writing workshop and afternoon enrichment class because the text is rich with colorful images, writing ideas, and poems that will spark students' curiosity.

The mentor text I selected showcased writing that broke traditional writing norms by changing letter size to correspond with a word's definition, or even better, resorted to concrete poetry to change the shape of sentences and words. I showed students this poem from Wolf's book, giving them a chance to talk together about the purpose of writing things in a nontraditional way. "Would you be willing to try this with a poem of your own?" I asked. Some were hesitant, but they were willing to try.

Emily, one of the students in my enrichment group, worked meticulously on her poem, choosing a pencil as the topic and speaker of her poem. Her style of writing, blending concrete writing with her poem, made this a joy to read and use as a mentor text with my regular classes.

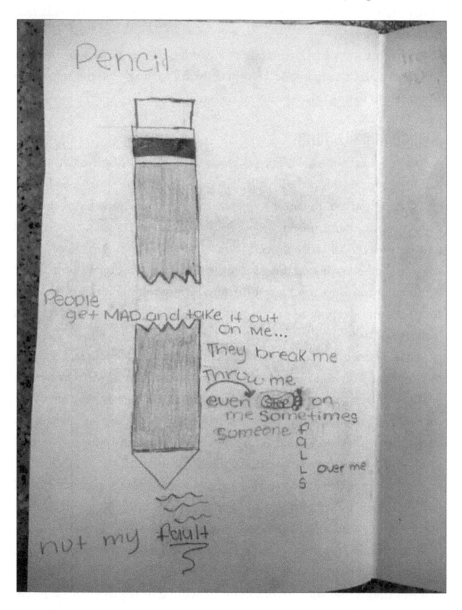

Different subject area teachers could use this format to fuse their content with different forms of poems. It is not trivial to allow students time to write from the perspective of a chemical in a science experiment or a number in a math problem. If pieces of an algebraic equation could speak to one another, what would they say? How could students capture those bits of conversation in a poem or piece of writing that abandons the traditional format of poetry?

If we want students to fall in love with writing, we have to give them time to be whimsical and to think creatively. Creative thinking builds their capacity for abstract thinking. First, show them mentors. Then give them time to create.

The Power of Memoir

As we mentioned in Chapter 7, memoirs are powerful tools to use with students. Experience humanizes. And it unites. One of the best ways we have found to get students writing is to get them writing about themselves. Many of the young people in our classrooms shoulder responsibilities we did not dream of in our youth. They see and hear things we know would horrify us, even as adults. But writers use past experiences as inspiration for writing, and we want our students to understand they can, too.

Never a Day without a Line

A writer writes. Teachers of writers write. To explore the world through writing is to adopt a writer's life. That is what we want for ourselves, for you, and for the students in our lives.

For the past several years, I (Travis) have read the works of Donald Murray, the writer-thinker-teacher whose work in the field of writing, and the teaching of writing, has influenced the lessons, ideas, and assignments I bring to my students. While coauthoring this book, two things about Murray have waited patiently in the back of my mind as I searched for the right place to put them.

First, Murray believed in the power of his daybook. "I usually write in the daybook the first fifteen minutes of the day before breakfast," he wrote. "And then I have it near me all day long. If something occurs to me

I make a note . . ." I read these words in *The Essential Don Murray: Lessons from America's Greatest Writing Teacher* several months ago, and now, as I write this paragraph, I am returning to them. Don Murray lived the life of a writer. He never went a day without a line, knowing that putting pen to paper each day helped develop his craft as a thinker, writer, and a teacher of writers.

Second, I have read multiple times about Murray's laminated note cards, ones with the phrase "Never a Day without a Line" printed on them. People would ask Murray how to become a good writer, and in response, he would hand them one of these cards. I never knew Murray, but many times, I wish I could have gleaned from his immense wisdom.

Students need to write each day, writing from poetry, their independent reading, and mentor texts. You can guide this process, but it has to be a daily one. Be the guide for your students. We challenge you to get a notebook, and as Penny Kittle tells us, ". . . go and fill yours. Then share."

THINGS TO THINK ABOUT AND TWEET

How can you share your personal stories or a memoir with your students (or colleagues)?

If you teach a subject other than ELAR, how can you utilize more mentor texts into your instruction? If you teach ELAR, how can you help those other subjects approach this?

How can we collaborate more with grade level and cross-grade level activities to grow all of us?

#SparksInTheDark

Year after year, the student shudders under a barrage of criticism, much of it brilliant, some of it stupid, and all of it irrelevant. No matter how careful our criticisms, they do not help the student.

—Don Murray

Chapter 10

Changing Course: Vision and Revision

AFTER WE'VE DISTURBED THE universe, where do we go from there? We love what Maya Angelou says, "When you know better, you do better." And that means changing course and doing things differently—taking time, just as in writing, to revise, edit, and rewrite our lessons and ideas. In short, we rethink everything.

Real writers and readers go in search of material that inspires them. They seek things that echo their personal experiences and will answer questions that haunt them. When students enter our classrooms, our job is to provide an environment where their reading and writing lives can flourish. Quality classes include time for students to read, write, talk, and think. These are actions that are irreplaceable in any classroom.

Destructive Reading and Writing

Most educators have been there at one point or another—that moment when a child needs a consequence and they jump straight to "write this sentence one hundred times" or "sit there and read your book in silence for thirty minutes." It's an easy consequence. But both of us have come to understand and realize that it truly isn't what's best for a child.

When teachers make reading or writing a form of punishment, they create a sense of dislike for those subject matters. You create students whose memories of reading and writing are not marked by joy and self-expression but annoyance, frustration, and shame. Their primary connection to those activities is forged through punishment.

As the principal of an elementary campus, I've (Todd) held after-school detention as a form of punishment for students. It was the you-wasted-your-class-time-with-poor-choices-so-I'm-going-to-waste-yours-after-school approach. When we started this consequence, we always had them write sentences. For whatever reason, we had this notion that making a child write, "I will make better choices," would actually influence them on a deeper level. What were we thinking?

After having some of my writing teachers come to me concerned that this consequence was fostering a dislike of writing in students, I took a step back to reflect. They were right. We were creating an atmosphere in which writing equaled punishment. It reminded me of how, back when I was a teacher, I would make my students read when the class was behaving poorly. But the first step in bringing about genuine change is understanding. After realizing what we were doing to our students, I was determined to figure out something else as an effective punishment.

That's when we moved to digging to the heart of the issues. Our after-school detention became a place of meditation and mediation. We had kids stop, evaluate, and think through their choices. We worked with them on understanding their emotions and how to react in situations. And you know what? Our discipline issues decreased. That never happened with the sentence-writing.

Teachers and administrators, it is important for us to continually reflect on everything we do as a campus. Whether it's our lunchroom procedures, playground rules, hallway expectations, or discipline, we must make sure our campus is making decisions that are best for children and not just easiest for adults. It might not be easy to think of a solution right away, but taking time to have open conversations about why we do the things we do can lead to helpful changes.

I (Travis) have been passionate about reading and writing since childhood, and one of my goals is to nurture that same passion in my students. I want them to see reading as a lifestyle and writing as a means of expression, and I want to watch them grow to love the artistry of both. A rich reading and writing life will carry our students far, providing them with skills that will sustain them academically. While I have them, I want the year to be full of rewarding experiences in both reading and writing. There is an exquisite joy when a self-proclaimed nonreader falls in love with a book. When a student who has long despised language arts writes a thoughtful poem related to a book he just read. When hyperactive teenagers silence each other as they prepare for independent reading during class. These are noteworthy, indelible moments, and I treasure them deeply.

> There is an exquisite joy when a self-proclaimed nonreader falls in love with a book.

Not long ago, I found myself engaged in a conversation with several coworkers who were planning a reward day for their classes. One teacher had told her students if they were not eligible to participate in the reward, they would be going into another classroom and would have to read. Her requirement bothered me on so many different levels. If her students didn't earn the reward, they would be reading, implying that reading was a punishment. I mentioned to this teacher that a room devoted to reading would be a reward for many young people, and it was wrong to vilify books by using them as punishment. She only chuckled and walked from the room.

Students in my classes have time to write and read every day and experiment with different genres and mentor texts that will guide them to be better readers and writers. I always use positive language when I discuss the act of reading because I know my attitude can affect my students' outlook. I never issue punishments for a refusal to read or when I notice students are not reading outside of class. When those behaviors come up, I use the independent reading time during class to have conversations with those students. I want to know why they aren't reading, if the book is not interesting to them, if they are confused by the plot, or if they can't relate to the characters and their situations. I have never—knock on wood—been unable to get a student invested in a book after such a conversation. It takes some work, but it is well worth the time spent in discussion. The same goes with writing. If students are struggling with voice, word choice or structure, I sit with them to resolve the issue.

My classes are structured in a way to give students time to read, study, craft, and share. I devote a specific twenty-minute period each day to independent reading. Students have a chance to read something of interest to them, and most choose a book from my classroom library. Afterward, we spend time sharing what we read, writing about what resonated, or describing our favorite scenes. In conferences, I ask students to think about books they have loved, knowing the tone associated with the word "love" is one of warmth and comfort. That's what I want students to experience when they read—book love.

Unfortunately, we have heard the conversations many times from educators about the tendency to engage students in reading and writing as a punitive measure. Some students have learned to loathe any kind of reading and writing because these beautiful activities have been reduced to worksheets and comprehension exercises. When we use language that belittles the act of reading, we do a disservice to our kids. We showcase, with our words, how little we value literature and written expression, and we do so to the detriment of the learning process. No student will develop a love of books and writing if we represent them this way.

As educators, it is our responsibility to truly build a love of learning within our students. But that love of learning can never be built if we take the easy way out and use any form of education as a punishment. We'll lose our students, one by one, if we destroy any love they could develop for these subjects. What's truly important is getting to the heart of the issue. And you can only do that by truly connecting with others and learning who they really are.

> We now have a quarter century of studies that document three findings:
> Literacy blooms wherever children have access to books they want to read, permission to choose their own, and time to get lost in them.
> —Nancie Atwell

Free-Choice, Independent Reading

As kids, we were both mesmerized by stories. When entranced by a delightful book, we spend hours devouring the narrative, getting lost in the world of the characters and wishing we could step into their world for just a moment. We've seen glimmers of fictional characters in our teachers, our classmates, and even our parents. Even though we loved to read, some of our reading joy was shattered during school. Many of the books we would bring with us to class were not appropriate or "leveled," a term we came to loathe. And the books without Accelerated Reader labels were off-limits because how would our teacher determine the points we would earn? Or the overall quality of the book if it wasn't AR-approved? Sometimes we tried to read those books anyway, hiding them behind a textbook or under our desk. When we were caught, the novels were snatched from our hands, or we were asked to put them away. In upper grades, there was never time for independent reading, and our choices were rarely discussed or encouraged. Sadly, school never helped either of us develop a reading life. Today, as a teacher and a principal, we want much more for the children in our classes. We want them to fall in love with reading.

We have spent time talking with several middle-school children in our lives, and their collective indictment about language arts classes is sobering, particularly because they qualify for advanced programs. In their classes, independent reading is done outside the classroom or completed in class to participate in incentivized reading programs. And we'll admit, in the past, we both have been guilty of denying our students independent reading time because we didn't believe our students would choose books that would meet our reading standards. We were wrong.

The benefits of free-choice, independent reading far outweigh any graphic organizer, worksheet, skill drill, or group conversations students are exposed to in our classrooms. Nothing nurtures students' love of reading and books like actual time to read, and free-choice reading is an optimal method. There isn't a single language arts teacher who would deny the importance of reading, but free-choice reading, the activity we relish as adults, becomes incredibly controversial when students are involved.

The implication is that student choice is not valued. When we trust students to make their own choices, the classroom environment changes dramatically. Students move from passive attendees to active participants. They also discover more about themselves and their reading identity because they are compelled by genres they thought they would dislike.

For example, Caroline spent most of the first semester reading great young adult literature, and her writing notebook was filled with drafts that spoke to her love of these books. When students finish a book, we always ask them, "What is your plan now?" We are curious what they want to read next, and if they don't know, we help them. Caroline wanted to read *To Kill a Mockingbird,* but she was afraid she wouldn't like it. It was a classic, and those books had turned her off from reading in the past. All she needed was a little help navigating the first several chapters until she could establish her interest. In the end, she fell in love with the story. And when we shared our favorite books at the end of the year, *To Kill a Mockingbird* was at the top of her list.

As teachers, we must value the reading choices our students make, and although we might not agree with them, we have to do our best to guide them to excellent books. Some students will enjoy books we dislike, but we have to respect their choices. This respectful learning environment might encourage them to read a classic, one they might devour in just a few sittings.

> **We must value the reading choices our students make, and although we might not agree with them, we have to do our best to guide them to excellent books.**

We often find ourselves amazed at the reading communities that populate our classrooms and the classrooms of teachers we work with over the course of a year. Students unite around authors they love— Andrew Smith, Sharon Creech, Shaun Hutchinson, and Nicola Yoon. They form groups based on their love of specific books—*Orbiting Jupiter* by Gary Schmidt, *To Kill a Mockingbird* by Harper Lee, *The Burn Journals* by Brent Runyon, and *Exit, Pursued by a Bear* by E.K. Johnston, *Hatchet* by Gary Paulsen, *Diary of a Wimpy Kid* by Jeff Kinney, and *Dog Man* and *Captain Underpants* by Dav Pilkey. These reading communities are organic, blooming on their own, and the classroom comes alive with conversations about books and authors and reasons why others should read them.

Mainly, students need time to discuss what they are reading with their classmates. As they talk about characters, themes, unanswered questions, or unexpected twists, they get to know their classmates in relation to the books. They hear what other students have enjoyed and disliked, and during these discussions, reading recommendations naturally occur. If you have different reading communities in your classroom, try weaving in and out of groups and listening for chances to slip into a conversation and catch a book recommendation.

In most classrooms, before students have the gift of free-choice reading, these reading communities do not exist. There are no lively conversations about the books being read in class because the teacher is the only one who is choosing them. When students have the chance to self-select their own reading material, engagement in that material increases. More often than not, students will fall in love with a book they have chosen, and ultimately, they will want to share the story with someone else. Readers naturally seek a community of other readers to share stories they love.

As students move through their academic careers, it is imperative they develop independence in their reading lives. While they will encounter material they can't negotiate on their own and will need an instructor's guidance, they will also need fluency in their reading lives to help them reach a place where they can confidently approach rigorous works. All students need exposure to Shakespeare, Milton, Hemingway, Austen, Eliot, Wharton, Lessing, and a host of other great authors. But it's more important to help students fall in love with reading than to force them into the reading experiences traditionally deemed worthy of study.

It's important to have expectations about our classroom libraries and the books our students read, but within those parameters, students must have choices, because choices lead to ownership of their education. We both have asked our students to identify the things that make class enjoyable for them, and they consistently say being able to select their own reading materials made a difference in the effort they put forth in class.

For example, Jose, a student whose energy had frustrated teachers before, explained that he loved to read but rarely found teacher-selected texts interesting. He adored the opportunities to choose his own books and spent hours meticulously arranging images and words on every book talk presentation he created for class. He explained that the book talk presentations were a favorite of his, and he hoped he would have the chance to do more of them next year. When students own their learning, they take it seriously.

Your students are counting on you. They aren't waiting for you to get it right. They are moving to the next grade level, graduating, entering college, and accepting jobs. So, take some time to reflect on your regular practices. Are you providing students with time to read, reflect, and discuss? Are you promoting a classroom environment that allows students ample time to find books they are interested in and get lost in them? We believe in the power of free-choice reading because we have seen its potent magic in our classrooms and the classrooms of others.

Students weave beautiful stories about the things they love, and when they fall in love with books, those stories are magnified. We need a nation, a world of readers, and we can help build them. We encourage you to fill your classroom with books that students will love and allow everyone a chance to select the ones they want to read. Then, allow them to get comfortable, whether it's in their seats or a cozy place on the floor, and disappear into the narrative they have chosen. This is how you create readers.

> If you want to enhance their worldviews.
> you have to let them share their ideas.

We find the best language arts and social studies classes are structured in a way that gives students a chance to read, write, and share every day. If you want students to read, you have to let them read. If you want students to write, you have to let them write. If you want to enhance their worldviews, you have to let them share their ideas. All of this reading and writing and talking about reading and writing is not a waste of time. It's building students' abilities and sustaining their work as readers and writers.

THINGS TO THINK ABOUT AND TWEET

How can you develop passionate reading
communities in your classroom?
Or before or after school?

How can you restructure your classroom
to provide time for reading, writing,
and sharing each day?

How have you used or seen others use
reading or writing as punishment or a
negative consequence? How could you
change that practice?

What's a piece of writing that affects you
deeply? If you shared it with your students,
what would you tell them about it?

#SparksInTheDark

Let yourself be drawn by the pull of what you love. It will not lead you astray.

—Rumi

Chapter 11

The Noble Heart of a Teacher

FOR ME (TRAVIS), THE summer months are full of energy and drive. During this time away from school, away from the minutiae that often dominates education, I recharge and regroup for another year of helping develop the reading and writing lives of young people. Preparing for a new year is exciting and overwhelming. Like many educators, I spend hours agonizing over the best ways to motivate and encourage students, and each summer I remind myself I'm preparing lessons for students I don't yet know. Some of those students will enter my classroom excited about the new year, while others will still be shaking off the frustrations of the last one. Many will arrive in my classroom with challenges I might not understand and issues I might spend the entire year trying to solve. Regardless of their attitudes toward my subject area or the circumstances that might have impeded their academic journeys, one thing is for certain: I will love them.

I have faith that every student in my classroom will succeed. Without a doubt, these young people are equipped with the ability to write with vigor and read with passion. Loving my students means working hard to reverse the negative feelings they might have about my content area. Part of this profession involves a commitment to the resistant students, the kids who have fallen out of love with learning and are content just to survive.

We all have those students. They're the ones who will push all of our buttons, who will fight us at every turn, and who will make us wonder if we have what it takes to reach them. They're the students who touch our hearts and stick with us for a lifetime. They're students like . . .

John

When John walked into my (Travis) class, hair swept across his eyes, he was entirely uninterested in school or reading. I know because he told me. The explanation I gave him about independent reading in my classroom was a waste of time. It was an expectation he had no intention of meeting. Regardless of the books I handed him and the recommendations I made, he was not compelled to read beyond the school day. During independent reading time, he would stare into the distance, and I knew he was miles away from class. Eventually, I learned that before he had moved to our school district, a close friend of his had committed suicide. For him, school was a hideous reminder of his friend's death, and in response, he resisted anything academic. But beneath the caustic comments and the baggy clothes that shrouded his thin body, there was a child with a unique personality and interests and passions still to unlock. As his teacher, I was responsible for his learning, and I was determined to reach him.

During a quick write one day, in response to photographs from World War II, I noticed him writing feverishly for the allotted two to three minutes. When I read his entry later, his clarity and knowledge about military history astounded me, and when I approached him with a preview stack, he selected *Unlikely Warrior: A Jewish Soldier in Hitler's*

Army by George Rauch. Although John still refused to read outside of school, and though I wished he would read voluminously, he read that book and loved it. Ultimately, the expectation that students read independently outside of class was less important than helping John find a book he could enjoy, so I pushed the expectation aside. I don't regret it.

Catherine

Catherine, a young girl whose fiery eyes and anger told the story of intense heartache, despised writing. When I encouraged her to join the rest of the class during our writing workshop, she took it as a mere suggestion. But things changed when we started a study of memoir. Catherine chose to write about the death of her father, a man who had provided stability. In his absence, she suffered under the inattentive care of her mother. She cried while she wrote and twice asked to change the subject of her memoir, but in the end, she crafted a beautiful portrait of her father. Catherine's story resonated with me, and afterward, when the narrative had spilled onto the page and was no longer trapped inside her, she was a different person. In a note to me, she mentioned that no one had ever asked her to write about something so personal, but she was glad she had. So was I.

> No one had ever asked her to write about something so personal, but she was glad she had.

Jenny

Not all students are resistant. Jenny, for example, came to my class hating to read. Her reading inventory was filled with short answers, and only half of the inventory was actually completed. I knew right away this was a student who had concluded she wasn't a reader just for the simple fact that she had not found a book that had spoken to her soul, that had broken her heart, or had moved her. She had never met characters whose stories lingered in her thoughts for days after she had finished the book. But by the end of the year, her reading list contained more than thirty books and included more than five different genres. Books such as *Orbiting Jupiter* by Gary Schmidt, *Brown Girl Dreaming* by Jaqueline Woodson, and *Suicide Notes from Beautiful Girls* by Lynn Weingarten were part of her journey into discovering who she was as a reader. Her voracious reading habit, one that was only improved in my room, put my reading rate to shame.

Scott

Scott fell asleep in class almost every day. I (Todd) took away his chair, had him do jumping jacks, even called home to talk to his parents. I tried everything, but he continued to fall asleep. One day I decided to do something completely different with Scott. I rode the bus home with him, got off at his stop, and made a home visit. He introduced me to his family, we played some basketball out on the court, and I even helped him make his bed. Upon seeing his home, I understood why he was falling asleep in class every day. The bed we made was located in a room he shared with four of his cousins—all under the age of seven. They all slept in one bed. The kitchen didn't have a working refrigerator, and the carpet had been partially ripped up in the living room. Yet Scott didn't seem to mind showing me these spaces. He beamed when he talked about having to cook dinner each night for his cousins, aunt and uncle, two grandparents, and his mom and dad. He had been given the task because of health issues with the other family members and a few other factors. The next morning at school, Scott stopped me first thing to say "thank you." He said no one had ever shown any interest in where he lived, and it meant a lot to him. Scott didn't stay awake every day from then on, but he stayed awake some days! And he sure tried harder than ever before.

Book Love

These students' love of books was only magnified with the time and space to read and the opportunity to feel heard and valued. All of these students have one thing in common: They were accepted without question. They were given the freedom to find books they found interesting, topics they could develop through writing, and time to talk about both. We find ourselves worrying every year about the messages we send to our students. Kids are smart, more intuitive than we give them credit for being, and it is often the implications that send the strongest messages. When we say we love our students, it means showing them through our remarks, the things we advocate, and the assignments we ask them to complete. Our actions reflect our philosophies far more clearly than our words. Worksheets and chapter quizzes do not engender a love of reading or writing, and when we use them, students disengage. Loving our students means allowing them to participate in the activities of real readers and writers. It means giving them the power to choose and allowing them a chance to discover themselves through reading and writing.

> When we say we love our students,
> it means showing them through our
> remarks, the things we advocate, and the
> assignments we ask them to complete.

As educators, we give our all for our students. They become like our own children. We laugh and eat together. We give up hours of our time to help them. We lose sleep over their behavior, and our hearts break alongside them. And just about every year, there's that one student we work tirelessly to reach. Academically and emotionally, we throw everything we have at them. Every time-honored tool and every research-based practice we've learned along the way. But no matter how hard we try, we get nowhere. In those moments, many of us blame ourselves. We think, "What am I missing that I can't reach this child?" or "Do they not see how much I care or how hard I'm working for them? Why won't they meet me half-way?"

When many of us start out in education, we tend to believe—even if we don't say it aloud—it's our job to save every student given to us. On some level, we must know this is an impossible task, but we still internalize that burden. For years, I (Todd) certainly did. Then an educator I greatly respected told me, "You can't save every child that comes into your classroom. And that's not your job. Your job is to love them and educate them to the best of your ability." His words lifted such a weight off my shoulders. I finally understood I wasn't a failure just because I hadn't saved all my students. But let me be clear—I didn't take what he said as a reason not to try my hardest for every student. In that respect, I never let myself off the hook. It's still my responsibility to give everything I have to my students.

I think of education like planting a field. It requires many hands. Some of us till the soil, and some of us drop the seed. Some water those seeds daily, and some watch it grow and harvest the fruits of our labor. But none of us has to be all of those people. That's a hard thing for those of us who are elementary educators. So often, we till the soil and plant the seed, but we don't always see the growth. That was made even more clear to me when a student from my first year of teaching, more than eight years before, reached out to me for the first time since leaving my classroom. He was graduating from high school and wanted me to know the impact I had left on him when he was in fourth grade. He was a student I had worked tirelessly with but never felt like I had reached.

So, please, don't give up. If you're exhausted and losing hope—and it's okay to feel that way—take a deep breath before throwing in the towel. Take a breath and love your students. Show up every day, and hand them a clean slate. Don't just tell your students you love them, show them. Lean on your colleagues. Try new things.

The children you teach each year will arrive with unique stories, quirks, and needs. Because you love this profession and the students you teach, you will do everything in your power to make it a memorable and worthwhile school year. We're all planting this field together, and whether we sew the seed or harvest the crop, it's our job is to educate and love these children.

We Are All Immigrants

I (Travis) was immobilized the day I read the news that Muslim refugees from select countries had been banned from entering our country; I knew I could not accept the brutal attack on refugees in our country, and I must rage against such ideology.

The injunction, issued from the highest office in the United States, was a response that, from my perspective, was driven by fear, self-service, racism, and ignorance. I was stunned by the way many people disregarded the egregious attack on humanity, seemingly indifferent to the prejudice that had prompted the decision. Images of war-torn countries, starving children, and ravaged landscapes infiltrated my mind, especially when I heard others justifying the actions of our president. Even now, I am mortified.

> Reading makes immigrants of us all.
>
> —Jean Rhys

We live in a nation where values are quickly eroding, where signatures on knee-jerk executive orders have the power to shatter countless lives. The pen is, indeed, mightier than the sword. We cannot begin to understand these destructive notions that have superseded logic and reason, and we worry about the outcome for our students. Their minds are so impressionable, and they are witnessing actions that vilify entire cultures and minority groups. As in times past, we find ourselves turning to books for solace, understanding, and to continually build empathy.

Reading is a curious act. Current research suggests that reading helps us develop empathy; our brains are stimulated as though we were actually experiencing the activity in the book. Jean Rhys, a contemporary novelist, was accurate when she noted that reading causes all of us to be immigrants because the act of reading is a journey of the mind. Books offer chances to travel, providing a passport to distant lands that we may not be able to physically experience, but our minds are given the free-dom to explore them. We dwell in possibilities when we read.

When you read a book like *The Cellist of Sarajevo* by Steven Galloway, it transports you to Bosnia, a country where life is extinguished by bul-lets that rip through the air with searing, fatal precision. You're able to see the courage of people living their lives in the face of war, who know they aren't guaranteed tomorrow but who have resolved to keep going. A story like *A Thousand Splendid Suns* by Khaled Hosseini can engulf you in the rich culture of the Middle East, where you witness life through the eyes of two women who are enduring the hardship of a patriarchy. You are gifted with the opportunity to hear their questions and sense their uncertainties. Viet Thanh Nguyen's *The Sympathizer* carries you to Vietnam, and you experience struggles with loyalty and searches for meaning. These novels make immigrants of us all.

As Rhys so astutely observed, every time we read, we are foreigners. We are the strangers, the aliens, the wanderers. Standing in the shoes of a complete stranger, we see how life in that world functions. For a moment in time, we are guests in another world, and even when reading fiction, our brains authenticate the experience through sensory reactions. We experience life with a traumatized father in Laurie Halse Anderson's *The Impossible Knife of Memory*, while *Feed* by M.T. Anderson enables us to feel heartache and confusion, seeing the world through augmented real-ity. Kwame Alexander's *The Crossover* gifts us with a chance to view the world through an African-American adolescent's eyes, witnessing failure and triumph. *All Rise for the Honorable Perry T. Cook* by Leslie Connor shares stories of people whose choices have landed them behind bars but who can be defined by something other than their mistakes. With novels like *Ninth Ward, Towers Falling,* and *Sugar,* Jewell Parker Rhodes brings to life historical moments—and the people who lived through them—such as Hurricane Katrina, the 2001 World Trade Center attacks and slavery on a Louisiana plantation. *The Alex Crow,* by Andrew Smith, weaves multiple perspectives to recount a refugee's haunting past and his resilient acceptance of an unexpected future. These books teach us what it means to be human. They allow us momentary glimpses into the lives of characters who, although fictional, are representations of all of us.

When we read to understand, we are better able to champion the immigrant who traveled thousands of miles to create a new life for herself. We are more likely to sympathize with the frustrated child who faces paralyzing horror at home. And we can welcome the refugee who is simply seeking a safe haven from the terror of a distant land.

Fear is the enemy of wisdom.

Our reading lives make us an immigrant, and each time we pick up a book, we not only hope to get lost within the narrative, but we also wish to seek deeper understanding. Fear is the enemy of wisdom. We do not want our students to be afraid of people or ideas that are different than the ones they hold sacred. We want them to read to acknowledge cultural differences and to develop an understanding of culture, people, life, and acceptance. We must teach them books are powerful weapons against ignorance, and as readers, we must educate ourselves with narratives of humanity from across the globe. We are guests in the world of the book, and we are always welcome.

THINGS TO THINK ABOUT AND TWEET

Think about that child you did not feel you were able to reach. How can you keep it from eroding your resolve to continue giving your best to all students?

When was a book love developed in you? What novel or story did you first connect with on a deeper level?

How can you and your colleagues share your own book love with students in a way that feels genuine and honest?

How can you use stories in your classrooms and with your colleagues to build empathy?

#SparksInTheDark

The essence of teaching
is to make learning
contagious, to have one
idea spark another.

—Marva Collins

Chapter 12

From Whom Do We Learn?

WE'RE ALL LEARNERS, AND we should be growing ourselves every day. We ask our students to show up every day ready to learn—and to stick with it, through all the ups and downs, for at least twelve years. Yet as adults, how committed are we to that same learning adventure? Do we complain about that new tool our district is making us learn? Do we only go to training once or twice a year and consider ourselves fully developed, professionally speaking? If we expect our students to take learning seriously, we have to show them none of us ever stops learning.

While writing this book, we thought about different ways to continue growing, learning new skills, challenging our beliefs and opinions. Here's our short list:

Learning through Social Media

Social media has completely revolutionized the way we interact as individuals. Whether it's Facebook, Instagram, Twitter, Voxer, or a plethora of other tools, we are now able to connect more often—and more easily—than ever before in history.

Connecting through social media is also something very personal to both of us because that's exactly how we met. This book wouldn't exist today had it not been for a chance encounter on Twitter that led to us following each other's writing and discovering a commonality between our beliefs and a shared love of reading and writing.

In some ways, social media is the great equalizer. It affords educators across the globe the ability to connect with one another, share their practices and ideas, and learn from others who are doing the same. That intrinsic benefit is what's so exciting! Because these educators are on social media, they're clearly looking to connect and grow too.

We no longer can claim ignorance.

I (Todd) could list a thousand different ways being on social media has changed my life, not only professionally but also personally. If it weren't for Twitter, I wouldn't have the principal job I have now, wouldn't have met President Barack Obama, wouldn't have created *Kids Deserve It!* or *Stories from Webb*, and so much more. Don't get me wrong—social media can feel overwhelming and be a scary place to share your ideas. I constantly face feelings of doubt and insecurity when I log on and see some of the incredible things other educators and leaders are doing. If I'm not careful, I start to compare myself to others and believe my own ideas aren't that great. That's when I have to remind myself I am bringing something special to the field of teaching and force myself to share my insights with the world. After all, what might seem ordinary to me could be eye-opening and magnificent to someone else.

When I travel and speak constantly about connecting on social media, one question I continually face is, "How do you have time for social media?" My response? I make time, whether that's in the checkout line at the grocery store, five minutes before heading home from work, during commercials while watching TV, or even ten minutes before going to bed. I take just a few minutes a day to learn something from others online. I also commit to at least one Twitter chat a week or a month during which I focus time on a specific topic that forces me to connect with others and push my own thinking. An important note— when I schedule the time, it's much more likely to happen!

Connecting on social media is a learning process. With the ability to Google any answer to a question we don't know—What is a hashtag? or How do I Tweet a photo?— we no longer can claim ignorance. We have at our disposal tools that are free of charge and accessible twenty-four hours a day. No more excuses.

Learning from Students

One thing we've learned throughout our years in education is that we learn more from our students than anywhere else. When we take the time to truly listen to and work alongside our students, we can learn from them in ways that are unpredictable and that have the power to change the whole dynamic of our classrooms, instruction, and our own beliefs about teaching.

For me (Todd), being a connected educator has changed everything. No longer do I work in a silo surrounded by ideas that are limited based on my location or experience. Because I have chosen to connect with and learn from educators from around the world, I have had my eyes opened on many occasions. Those experiences have also made me better for my students.

One of the most powerful lessons I've learned is the importance of providing students with books that have characters who look like them.

Characters who talk like they do and who live like they do. As a white kid raised in a white family, I was surrounded by books with white characters, people who looked and talked like me and everyone I knew. I never thought twice about it. When I became an educator, and later a campus leader, I continued not to think twice about the books and characters I was sharing with my students. In time, after hearing what respected peers had to say about the value of diverse characters and stories, I gave my go-to reading material a hard look. In general, the characters were predominantly white and male. It wasn't an intentional choice, but it happened. And it was a problem because eighty percent of my students are not white. I knew I could do better by my students, so I spent an entire summer diversifying my library. I read *Towers Falling* and *Ninth Ward* by Jewell Parker Rhodes, *Mexican WhiteBoy* and *Last Stop On Market Street* by Matt de la Peña, *Booked* and *The Crossover* by Kwame Alexander, and so many more.

Then something special happened. Several things, really, because of a few very different books.

In my effort to branch out, I also worked hard at choosing more diverse picture books. As a principal, it's my responsibility to make monthly visits to every classroom on campus to read to students. I prefer to read a book that has touched my heart or captivated my imagination, and from prekindergarten to fifth grade, it's one of my favorite activities.

With my newfound awareness, I screwed up my courage and decided to step outside my comfort zone. More than half of my students speak Spanish, and we have bilingual classes in prekindergarten through third grade. I recently had discovered *How Do Dinosaurs Stay Friends?* by Jane Yolen and loved it, and when I saw the Spanish version, *¿Cómo son buenos amigos los dinosarios?*, everything clicked! I practiced reading it with a friend who speaks Spanish, and I surprised each bilingual classroom, reading to students in their native language. The shock was clear on their little faces, and while the youngest giggled quite often at my pronunciation, the older students were proud to help me out. It was such a fun experience, and the students truly enjoyed having their principal read to them in their language.

Then I took my next step. The picture books by Andrea Beaty—*Rosie Revere, Engineer* and *Iggy Peck, Architect*—are some of my favorites, and she had just released her newest one, *Ada Twist, Scientist*. It's an amazing story, written in verse, about a young African-American girl and the many scientific questions she asks to learn more and more. Roughly one-third of our students are African-American, and I wanted to read to them from a book that reflected their experiences instead of mine. They loved it. I read *Ada Twist, Scientist* with class after class. They laughed, they clapped, and we had lively talks about the story. But it was an encounter in the hallway the next day that forever changed the way I view the books I choose to read to classrooms. A young girl, who was in the fourth grade, stopped me and said, "Thank you, Mr. Nesloney, for reading that book to our class yesterday." Of course, I told her it was my pleasure and that I loved reading to all the classes. Then she added, "No, thank you for reading a story where she looked like me. Someone who was my color and who did something great." It was hard to hold back tears. I just gave the girl a hug and let her continue on her way, but her words will never leave me. They validated everything I learned that summer.

"Thank you for reading a story
where she looked like me."

When we choose to celebrate where our students come from and who they are, we connect with them on a deeper level and foster empathy and a safe environment. To learn from our students, we have to talk to them—whether a regular morning meeting, a weekly Google form seeking feedback, or an anonymous tip box. Yes, it is a scary thing to open ourselves up to feedback from students, but we want our classrooms to be a place where students thrive, we must stop and listen as often as we talk.

We must offer, read, and celebrate books that broaden our students' lives. That means exposing them to stories with characters who reflect their surroundings, who talk, look and act like them as well as stories with characters who are talk, look and act nothing like our students. We are educators, and it's our responsibility to shine a light and celebrate the diversity that exists within our schools, countries, and world.

Learning from Each Other

We can't forget the power of learning from those we work next to every day on our campuses and all across our school districts. It is so important that we make time to connect with, share with, and challenge our colleagues. When this conversation is broached, the quick response is often, "I already plan with my team, and we're completely aligned." But we want to look at this from another angle altogether.

It's easy for teachers to become isolated within their individual silos. Think about it. When was the last time you planned a collaborative lesson or activity with a colleague from a completely different grade level or content area?

I (Todd) have tried to provide opportunities at my school for teachers in different grades and subjects to work together. One particularly fun day, I walked down our second-grade hallway only to find our fifth-grade students doing the teaching. Groups of fifth graders had pulled aside groups of second graders and were teaching them the steps to the water cycle—knowledge both groups had to master, according to their state standards. The fifth graders had prepared great visuals and were going through all the steps, allowing the second graders to ask questions (and you know second graders, they always have questions). The second graders then were asked to write about what they had learned from their small-group leaders, and each fifth grader partnered with a second grader to assist with edits after they had completed the rough drafts.

For weeks, the fifth graders talked about the activity, and when both grade levels took their exams, the largest percentages in years earned passing grades. Though test scores should never be the sole focus of what we do, activities such as this one can truly empower students to take charge of and share their learning.

Research has shown us the importance of having students teach each other and how much that practice increases their own understanding of a concept. When you can kill two birds with one stone—combine different grade levels to cover multiple standards with one activity—it seems like a win-win to us.

It's also imperative that we don't spend all of our time alone in our classroom, connecting only with educators online, or only planning with our content and grade-level teams. We must take a risk, put ourselves out there, be brave, and collaborate and plan with other grade levels and content areas. It will benefit our students and help us grow as learners and teachers.

And administrators, this is for you too! You need to get into classrooms and team-teach with your teachers, taking on a full lesson or pulling out students for small-group tutoring. This is a great way for administrators to continue their own learning without simply reading a book or attending a training. It allows you to get down in the trenches with teachers and stay current on what's really happening in the classroom. We need leaders who realize that being an instructional leader is just as important as being a campus manager, and you can't be an instructional leader while hiding behind a computer from the comfort of your office.

Learning from Family

In the process of writing this book, I (Todd) unexpectedly lost my mother, Sally Rost (to whom this book is dedicated). Let me tell you a little bit about her. My parents divorced when I was in sixth grade, and my younger brother and I moved with my mom back to Brenham, Texas (where I still live today). My mother had always been a stay-at-home mom as we grew up and only had taken one semester of college classes. She worked cleaning houses and attending night school while my brother and I went to school. My brother decided to move in with my dad a year or two later, but me being the mama's boy (no shame here), I stayed with her. I don't know how she did it, but she paid her whole way through college, took care of us, cleaned houses, and graduated with almost perfect grades. She was determined. She was my hero and graduated college with her education degree exactly three years before I did. She got a job teaching fourth-grade reading and writing in Somerville, Texas, and worked there for the next thirteen years.

I always wanted to be half the teacher my mom was. She always worked with kids who came from difficult backgrounds. She purchased almost everything in her classroom, not to mention she earned a salary that was almost $10,000 less than the district I was teaching in. But she loved it because it completed her. She poured her heart and soul into those students every single day. And when I spent time with my mother, the entire conversation was about what was going on in her classroom.

> She poured her
> heart and soul into those
> students every single day.

Then 2018 arrived. Mom had been suffering from shortness of breath and high blood pressure for a while. But being the hard-headed woman that she was, she refused to see a doctor. Finally, after not being able to take it anymore, she went to an express clinic to see what was going on. The doctors couldn't really see anything majorly wrong, but they advised her to go see a specialist. Three weeks later, her symptoms persisted.

Mom just hated leaving work. She was the first teacher at school every morning and the last one there every night. She also worked every weekend I can remember, but unbeknownst to the family, she couldn't even walk from her classroom to the workroom without having to stop and take a break, her principal and superintendent made the decision that she couldn't come back until she saw a doctor. That was on a Wednesday.

The very next day (Thursday), she was still suffering, and while talking with her sister (my aunt) on the phone, she asked my aunt to take her to the emergency room. By the time my aunt arrived at the house, my mom couldn't even walk to the car. The ambulance was called, and they took her straight to the hospital in Brenham. My wife and I quickly rushed over. Mom was in great spirits and was acting like her normal smart-aleck self. The doctors' only concern was that they could not get her blood pressure or heart rate down no matter what medicine they tried. Thinking it wasn't a big deal, my wife and I headed home.

The next morning my aunt called me to tell me they moved my mom to a larger hospital in a nearby town. They had found two large blood clots overnight, one in each lung. And they still couldn't get her heart rate or blood pressure down. My aunt ordered my brother and me to go to work like normal because they were all just sitting around, waiting on a doctor.

At 2:25 that Friday afternoon, my aunt texted us all that whatever medicine they had tried had an adverse effect and dropped her blood pressure to dangerously low levels. I rushed home, grabbed my wife, and we went straight to the hospital. When we got there, my mom was groggy but still being funny and talking. The doctors said they would just keep her there, watch her heart rate, and get those blood clots dissolved with the aid of some blood thinners.

It was the start of my spring break and my birthday was in two days, and my wife and I had booked my dream trip to Jamaica over a year ago. My mom told us we better not cancel and that she would be out of that hospital in a day or two, so we had better not miss our flight. During the last conversation before our trip, we all laughed about Mom's beloved dog that my wife and I were taking care of and how the nurses were treating my mother.

Little did I know that was the last words I would speak to her.

My wife and I, trusting my mom and what the doctors were telling us at the time, drove to Dallas to spend the night to catch our flight the next morning. On Saturday we boarded our flight because there had been no changes overnight. But when we landed for our connection in Florida, I received a phone call from my aunt telling me that everything had gotten significantly worse. My mother had coded on the table and doctors had to do CPR to revive her. Her heart had become incredibly weak, her liver had given out, and her kidneys were failing. I remember feeling like what

I was hearing was some giant joke. I couldn't breathe. I couldn't speak. My wife and I walked right off the plane and fifteen minutes later, we boarded a plane back to Texas.

When we arrived back at the hospital, we discovered my mom had been placed in a medically induced coma. They were trying to protect her body and hoping to slowly wake her the next day. I remember walking into her room and seeing tubes and machines everywhere. The woman on the bed looked nothing like my mother. Machines were breathing for her and medicines were being pumped throughout her body.

Sunday came, and they decided they weren't ready to wake her back up yet because they wanted to continue to let her body heal. So, I spent my birthday in the hospital waiting on my mom to wake up.

Monday came, and the doctors began to wake her, a process that takes hours. After about five hours of being off sedation, the doctors decided to place her back under because they felt she was getting too agitated and that her heart was still trying to work too hard. They told us they would try again on Tuesday.

I remember walking into the hospital with the biggest hope on Tuesday morning. I went in and saw my mom, looking just the same— hooked up to everything. But I just had this gut feeling today was going to be a great day. Three hours later, my world crashed around me.

Mom's doctor came out and told us he had bad news. My mother's heart and kidneys were not improving. In fact, they were getting worse because of the clots. He informed us that they found out my mother had sleep apnea. Since it had never been diagnosed or treated, it had weakened her heart for years. When the two blood clots hit her lungs, her heart just couldn't handle it. He explained that they had an idea for a procedure that they could do at a hospital a few hours away. They would call the doctors over there to investigate if it could be successful. He told us to be cautious in our hope; my mother's body was very fragile and because of all the places they had poked to give her medicine, they couldn't give her the specialized treatment to remove the clots immediately because she would bleed out.

An agonizing forty-five minutes passed, and the doctors called us into a small room. (You know when they do that, the news isn't good.) They told us that doctors at the other hospital said that, with her vitals the way they were, the operation wouldn't work. She needed a heart transplant, but because of her state, she wasn't even a candidate for one. The doctors told us we had to make a choice. And me, being her oldest son, *I* had to make a choice.

I could choose to allow them to do a surgery that had a less than ten percent chance of working, and if it worked, would give her a life that would be drastically different than the one she had been living before, or I could allow them to take her off life support. When the doctor told me she had a ninety percent chance of bleeding out and suffering a very painful death during the surgery, I knew what I had to do. And when he said that if it was his mother or daughter, he would not put them through that agony, it made it even more clear to me. I sat there in the room with my wife, my aunt, and my grandmother. My grandmother slowly came to the sad realization that she was about to lose her second child, after already burying two husbands. I sat there as my aunt processed the fact she was about to lose another sibling.

I remember telling them I needed to call my brother, and I slowly left the room. It was like a movie where everything seems unreal. Where I was seeing the world through someone else's eyes. I found a seat and called my brother. I cried while filling him in and he told me, "Todd, you know what to do. I trust you." I told him to get here as soon as possible, and we would wait until he arrived. I then returned to where my family was, now sitting in the waiting room, and broke the news. We were going to take Mom off life support.

We sat there, and we cried. We broke. I felt my entire world shatter around me. Two days after I turned thirty-three, I found myself saying goodbye to the woman who raised me and made me the man I am today.

Over the next several hours, while we waited for my brother to arrive, my uncle and one of my cousins came up as well to say good-bye. My mentor, Troy Sikes, also showed up. He was my youth pastor, then my pastor, and the man who married my wife and me. He has been like a father to me. He held me and let me cry, he prayed over me, and he provided much-needed words of wisdom.

When my brother arrived, we could barely speak. We informed the doctors of our decision. Having never been through anything like this before, we didn't know what would happen next or how long any of this would take.

I remember them calling me, my brother, and our wives back to the room to be there. They had just taken her off all support, and she was breathing, very laboriously, on her own. We sat there, and we cried. Again. We held her hand. We rubbed her arm. It was the most painful experience of my entire life. I remember leaning over her and saying, "Mom, we're here. We're all here. It's okay." Her eyes barely flitted open in that moment, her ragged breathing stopped, and everything was over. It was like she was waiting for me to tell her we were there, so she could let go. When the doctors came into the room to tell us she was gone, it was like the entire earth crumbled beneath my feet. I walked out of the room and into where family was to let them know it was over.

Over the next several days, I lived in a state of shock—my rock, my mother, was gone. Then my principal brain kicked in, and I realized she passed away during her spring break. So that upcoming Monday, when her students returned to class, they would only then learn that their teacher had passed away, and that broke me all over again.

Why do I share all of this? What does this have to do with a chapter about people we learn from? Because the lessons I learned from my mother are ones that I will never forget. My mother showed me what it looks like to fall in love with a book and that desire to talk about it with someone as soon as you were done reading it. She taught me how to love the students I serve with every ounce of my being. Mom also demonstrated how to forgive, how to teach, and how to love.

On March 13, 2018, two days after I turned thirty-three, my mother was reunited with her father and her brother. She was in no more pain, and she was free.

Every single second since that moment has been hard for me. I have wept, I have been angry, I have felt completely broken and like I couldn't even take my next breath. I have laughed over memories of my mother, but most of all, I've remembered the many things she taught me.

Mom may not be here with me today, but she lives on through me. And I have made it my personal mission that her story will live on because I will tell it everywhere I go. That led me to start a new video series on Facebook called "Tell Your Story" where I seek to amplify those personal stories of others (with her story being the first one I shared). It also led to the selling of t-shirts and donating all the proceeds to buy books for students at Title 1 schools, just as my mom would have wanted. My mother championed for others (and me) every day. Now I get to champion for the underprivileged, those forgotten, and work to give them a voice and support them, all in my mother's name.

Everyone needs a cheerleader. My grandmother and my mother were mine. From bragging about me to friends and family, to telling me I could be anything I wanted (even if it was an educator living on little to no money), or never letting me forget how loved I was because there was always an opportunity for them to say it out loud. I felt like I could conquer anything because my mother and grandmother told me I could. And because of that, I know that I will root for every single child I serve. I will remind them I love them, and I will tell them that they can vanquish any foe and climb any mountain because I might be the only one who tells them.

You write to discover what you want to say.
—Don Murray

Learning from Writing

The above quote is printed in large letters, pasted to construction paper, and stapled to the back wall of my (Travis) classroom. It serves as a constant reminder to my students and to me that writing gives birth to more writing. My notebook is filled with strikethroughs (I never scratch out anything, fearful I will eradicate a useful idea), marginalia, lists of words, sketches, and lesson ideas that have yielded articles, blog posts, presentations, and stories that have benefited my writing and teaching lives. As a writer, I need a storehouse of writing from which to draw, a place where thinking has started, ideas have formed, and sparks of stories illuminate pages. These bits of writing help build larger pieces that eventually turn into the things I publish on my blog, the pieces I share with other writers, and the stories and philosophy I have shared in this book. The more I write, the more I learn about writing. That is how writing works.

We understand how laborious writing is because, as writers ourselves, we participate in the process. We struggle to find precise wording, write the perfect segue, and craft the beautiful conclusion. And when our students fight the writing process because it is difficult, we understand them too. Writing is difficult, but the more we write, the better we understand ways to navigate tough situations in our writing.

Whatever the activity, whether playing sports, learning a musical instrument, or even something as simple as penmanship, we are never an expert our first time. No one masters a skill without quite a bit of practice and even more struggle and failure. The same can be said of our writing lives. If we aren't writing ourselves, attempting new genres, learning new vocabulary, tying in allegories, and so much more, how will our writing ever improve? As with any other skill, if we want to become better writers, we must write and write often.

And serious writers are never done growing. It's something they work at for the rest of their lives. In time, writers learn to trust their voices. They come to understand if they write and listen to their writing, as Don Murray eloquently advises, the writing will come.

Last school year, I (Travis) started a faculty writing group, asking educators in my building to join me once a week to write after school. I was not certain that many teachers would attend, but now, I have a solid group of teachers who show up each and every week. During this time, I might project a poem onto my whiteboard, photocopy an article that has resonated with me, or invite them to respond to the story that is thumping in their hearts. Whatever the prompt, I am always left amazed by their powerful words. It's not easy to write and share with your peers, especially when many of us are still so insecure about our writing abilities. I hear conviction in the voices of these teachers when they read their work aloud. Emotion flows freely, and when we are finished, they are pumped about returning the next week. I have witnessed increases in confidence, writing ability, and a desire to write more often. That is what writing does. This is why and how we learn from our writing.

> The point, I tell them and you, is to be in the game, to be at the table, to be a part of the conversation, to contribute what is yours to give to help all those who come along behind you, to not just be part of the story but to be one who helps write that story.
>
> —Jim Burke

Professional Reading Lives of Teachers

The scope of education is broad. From kindergarten to twelfth grade, students are immersed in literature, languages, history, mathematics, sciences, humanities, physical education, and the arts. Students spend thirteen years of their lives studying content to cultivate their minds. Our classrooms should be places of conversation, writing, critical thinking, and collaboration; together with students, we should discuss the larger issues in our world, using each content area as a lens to view those issues. Sadly, it is not happening.

We truly believe that teachers want to challenge their students. As beginners in the teaching world, we were adamant that our students read rigorous literature. We created multiple forms of assessments and hand-outs to distribute, certain that such activity would stimulate thought and provide a challenging learning experience for all our students. But as we have continued to grow as educators and reflective practitioners, we've consistently seen the error of our former practices and learned that more does not always equal better.

Giving students more information or more pieces to remember isn't true learning. It's a memory exercise. We do have a responsibility to help students develop their memory skills, but that alone does not broaden the mind. Reviewing content in class, then providing a chance to work problems in notebooks or complete more of the same ideas in groups is not bad teaching, but when that comprises the preponderance of a teacher's instructional practice, little is gained as far as mind cultivation goes. And students lose a year of true critical thinking. A teacher is the heartbeat of a classroom. Our decisions and talents guide our instruction, and if we expect a great deal from our students, we must expect even more from ourselves.

The first year I (Travis) attended the NCTE conference, my dear friend, Martha, and I waited in line to speak briefly with Kelly Gallagher, one of the strong thinkers in English education. I had a copy of his newest book, *In the Best Interest of Students*, tucked under my arm, eagerly waiting the moment he would sign it. When my turn came, he smiled as I approached his table. We shook hands, and I handed him my book. "How many years have you taught, Travis?" he asked as he inscribed the front page. "This is my eighth year," I said. He smiled again, handed me my book, and said, "Well, Travis, I'm glad you're here. I've found that the best teachers are the ones whose professional lives are as big as their teaching lives."

Although we spoke briefly, his words left an indelible mark, one that haunts me as I write this. Our professional lives are the significant force behind our students' success. The words and voices of these professional writers linger in my mind long after each school day. As I wade through stacks of papers, consider novels for book talks, think about my students' interests and how I can direct them to a more intense book love, the professional reading I have done is a touchstone to direct my thinking. At the foundation of every content area is literature that explains and extends the tenets of the subject. I know that we want what is best for our students, and in their best interest, it is important that we know the literature of our content areas and seek out other readings that will enhance what we already know.

> Our professional lives
> are the significant force
> behind our students' success.

Our greatest professional obligation is to our students. All teachers are responsible for providing sound instruction and continuing their education. We've often heard teachers say they see no reason to change lessons that have worked for years. We hear their point, but we also hear an excuse for stagnation. The professional reading life of a teacher requires responsibility, and it goes beyond an Internet search for lesson plans and information about content. The Internet is one of our largest resources, but it is not the only resource that informs our instruction. At this point in our careers, our lesson plans, ideas, and instruction are formed by the professional voices we have read (and continue to read), our experiences, and the content we know, as well as the process we use to deliver that instruction to students and fellow colleagues. There is so much talent among teachers, and we are confident this talent can be further developed by reading the writing of professionals in our fields.

Our suggestion? Find the strong voices and thinkers for your content area. Read the newest research about teaching your subject. Seek out conferences that will supply you with a deeper sense of your curriculum and renew your passion for teaching. We prioritize what we value, and when we do not value reading or learning, it shows. Our instruction is a mixture of what we have read, and when our reading lives are shallow, so is our teaching. It isn't an insult; it's the truth.

Our professional reading lives should be a light to others in our field, and together, we should build a community of thinkers, readers, and teachers to illuminate a path of understanding for our students. We challenge all teachers to begin a professional reading life, finding content-area literature that will enhance your teaching process. As reflective practitioners, we must seek out the best resources to cultivate ourselves and our students. If we aren't strong readers, we won't produce critical thinkers. Competency on an end-of-grade test is not proof that we have produced strong students, just that our students can take tests.

We realize most of you are pushed beyond reasonable limits at times. You are responsible for lesson plans, paperwork, assessments, grades, meetings, committees, differentiation, and bringing rigor to our classrooms (just to name a few). On top of that, you are parents, husbands, wives, children, community members, and leisure readers. Asking you to pull professional reading into a life already overflowing with responsibility is, we are sure, another burden. But if we didn't believe it would work, we wouldn't suggest it. Finding time to peruse websites and books related to your content area will make a significant difference in your teaching life and the success of your students. Finding even the smallest amounts of time will enhance the great things you are already doing. We have found the following suggestions to be helpful when looking to add professional material into our own reading lives.

- Set aside time one day each week to read professional materials on websites, especially national sites that have links to standards, lesson plans, and professional development. The information is free, and it uses technology most teachers already have in their classrooms.

- Find a professional book that correlates with a topic in your content area that you are passionate about. Determine how long it will take you to read it and set a personal goal for finishing.

- Reflect on your lesson plans and determine the type of professional material that would make your teaching even better. Write those ideas on your lesson plans so you have a goal.

- Seek out a reading community in your school. Even if it's just you and another teacher, it's better than being alone. Read the book together and discuss how it can be used to inform your teaching.

- Establish time for independent reading in your classroom. Read along with your students!

We have seen the benefit of our professional reading life in our classrooms and schools, and we are confident that you will see it in yours. We want nothing more than to support what is already happening in our classes. We are in this together, and we know we are working toward the same goal. What do you say? Will you help us write the story of success for our students and for everyone else who comes along? We'd love it if you would.

THINGS TO THINK ABOUT AND TWEET

Whom have you learned most from
in your career?

How have you utilized social media to
connect and learn? If you haven't,
what is holding you back?

Could you start a reading club with fellow
staff members? What book would you
choose first and how would you
get interest from others?

#SparksInTheDark

Read books.
Care about things.
Get excited.
Try not to be
too down on yourself.
Enjoy the ever present
game of knowing,

—Hank Green

Chapter 13

Gathering Resources

THROUGHOUT *Sparks in the Dark*, we have tried to provide you with ideas, excuse eliminators, strategies, research, and personal experiences that show just how powerful reading and writing—and the instruction of both—can be. As educators, we have to be the ones who can light a spark in children's hearts and help them fall in love with reading and writing.

We understand it can be overwhelming, and you might not be sure where to start. What we have tried do within this chapter is create for you a few lists of resources to help you out on your journey of being a spark in the darkness. These are resources that have influenced our teaching and leadership through the years. It is, by no means, a comprehensive list of all the books we have read or the ones worth reading. It's a starting place, offering a wide variety of options for your classroom and professional libraries.

Professional Books

- *Mechanically Inclined* by Jeff Anderson
- *In the Middle* by Nancie Atwell
- *The Reading Zone, 2nd Edition* by Nancie Atwell and Anne Atwell Merkel
- *Disrupting Thinking* by Kylene Beers and Robert E. Probst
- *The English Teacher's Companion* by Jim Burke
- *Joy Write* by Ralph Fletcher
- *Readicide* by Kelly Gallagher
- *Book Love* by Penny Kittle
- *Write Beside Them* by Penny Kittle
- *The Book Whisperer* by Donalyn Miller
- *Reading in the Wild* by Donalyn Miller
- *The Essential Don Murray* edited by Thomas Newkirk and Lisa C. Miller
- *Read to Write* by Donald M. Murray
- *The Art of Slow Reading* by Thomas Newkirk
- *Embarrassment* by Thomas Newkirk
- *Minds Made for Stories* by Thomas Newkirk
- *Read Write Teach* by Linda Rief
- *Seeking Diversity* by Linda Rief
- *Teaching Reading in Middle School* by Laura Robb
- *Blending Genre, Altering Style* by Tom Romano

Fiction and Nonfiction Books

- *Crash Course* by Kim Bearden
- *Between the World and Me* by Ta-Nehisi Coates
- *Out of My Mind* by Sharon Draper

- *For White Folks Who Teach in the Hood . . . And the Rest of Y'all Too* by Christopher Emdin
- *Born a Crime* by Trevor Noah
- *A Long Walk to Water* by Linda Sue Park

Picture Books

- *Whoosh!* by Chris Barton
- *The Princess and the Pony* by Kate Beaton
- *Ada Twist, Scientist* by Andrea Beaty
- *I Like Myself* by Karen Beaumont
- *Once Upon a Time . . . Online* by David Bedford and Rosie Reeve
- *Freedom in Congo Square* by Carole Boston Weatherford and R. Gregory Christie
- *The Legend of Rock, Paper, Scissors* by Drew Daywalt
- *The Day the Crayons Came Home* by Drew Daywalt and Oliver Jeffers
- *You Don't Want a Unicorn* by Ame Dyckman
- *Ribbit* by Rodrigo Folgueira
- *Red* by Michael Hall
- *Ralph Tells a Story* by Abby Hanlon
- *Mother Bruce* by Ryan T. Higgins
- *The Bad Seed* by Jory John
- *We Are Growing* by Laurie Keller
- *Anansi the Spider* by Gerald McDermott
- *Mango, abuelu y yo* by Meg Medina
- *One* by Kathryn Otoshi
- *My Name is Yoon* by Helen Recorvits
- *Creepy Pair of Underwear* by Aaron Reynolds
- *Happy Dreamer* by Peter H. Reynolds

- *The Adventures of Beekle; The Unimaginary Friend* by Dan Santat
- *After the Fall* by Dan Santat
- *The True Story of the 3 Little Pigs!* by Jon Scieszka
- *The Most Magnificent Thing* by Ashley Spires
- *Kenya's Art* by Linda Trice
- *What You Do with a Problem* by Kobi Yamada

Chapter Books for the Middle Grades (Fourth through Eighth Grades)

- *Dancing Home* by Alma Flor Ada
- *Booked* by Kwame Alexander
- *Ms. Bixby's Last Day* by John David Anderson
- *Wishtree* by Katherine Applegate
- *Nine, Ten* by Nora Raleigh Baskin
- *Code Talker* by Joseph Bruchac
- *Because of Mr. Terupt* by Rob Buyea
- *All Rise for the Honorable Perry T. Cook* by Leslie Connor
- *The Red Pencil* by Andrea Davis Pinkney
- *Into the Wild* by Sarah Beth Durst
- *Scar Island* by Dan Gemeinhart
- *Braced* by Alyson Gerber
- *Full Cicada Moon* by Marilyn Hilton
- *Ruby Lee and Me* by Shannon Hitchcock
- *Restart* by Gordon Korman
- *Rules* by Cynthia Lord
- *Fish in a Tree* by Lynda Mullaly Hunt
- *The Someday Birds* by Sally J. Pla
- *Esperanza Rising* by Pam Muñoz Ryan

- *Towers Falling* by Jewell Parker Rhodes
- *Ghost* by Jason Reynolds
- *The Gauntlet* by Karuna Riazi
- *When You Reach Me* by Rebecca Stead
- *Save Me a Seat* by Gita Varadarajan and Sarah Weeks
- *Blooming at the Texas Sunrise Motel* by Kimberly Willis Holt
- *Brown Girl Dreaming* by Jacqueline Woodson

Young Adult Books

- *Mexican WhiteBoy* by Matt de la Peña
- *Allegedly* by Tiffany D. Jackson
- *One of Us is Lying* by Karen M. McManus
- *Long Way Down* by Jason Reynolds
- *All American Boys* by Jason Reynolds and Brendan Kiely
- *I'm Not Your Perfect Mexican Daughter* by Erika L. Sánchez
- *Dear Martin* by Nic Stone
- *The Hate U Give* by Angie Thomas
- *The Sun Is Also a Star* by Nicola Yoon
- *The Serpent King* by Jeff Zentner
- *American Street* by Ibi Zoboi

Helpful Websites

- diversebooks.org
- ala.org (American Library Association)
- Edutopia.com
- goodreads.com (book reviews and reading suggestions)
- heinemann.com (provides helpful supplemental material)
- kellygallagher.org
- kylenebeers.com

- movingwriters.org
- nationalbook.org (reading lists and presenter of the National Book Award)
- pennykittle.net
- WeAreTeachers.com

THINGS TO THINK ABOUT AND TWEET

What are some of your favorite resources?

How can you make sure your resources feature diverse characters, authors, and stories?

Take some time to reflect on your own library of books? What's in the majority? What's missing altogether? What are some stories you would like to add?

#SparksInTheDark

I believe a lot of our lives are spent asleep, and what I've been trying to do is hold on to those moments when a little spark cuts through the fog and nudges you.

—Rufus Wainwright

Epilogue

Wanderer above the Sea of Fog by Caspar David Friedrich

In writing this book, we sought to encourage, challenge, inspire, question, and shift your thinking when it comes to reading and writing and instruction overall. We hope we have shown you glimpses of our hearts and our classrooms and schools as examples of what is truly possible when you start to believe in what was once thought as improbable.

As you venture back into your classrooms and school buildings, consider the painting on the previous page. It's a gorgeous image of a man standing upon a rock and staring into the unknown. A vast space, covered in a sea of fog. Much like that wanderer's view, our own paths will not always be clear. We might find them overgrown, rocky, and difficult to navigate. We might be fearful as we continue down roads we haven't yet explored and try things we never even imagined.

As you climb to the top of your educational mountain and gaze into the vast and great unknown, we hope you're filled with a little less apprehension and maybe a little more drive to be brave and charge on. To take the path less traveled. To beat back the overgrown excuses that have cluttered your way. To silence the voices that threaten to drive you back to the familiar.

We hope you take the small spark we have tried to illuminate within you and use it to light the way for your students. To keep walking. To keep taking risks and venturing towards the scary spaces. Take that spark, hold it close to you, and use it to light up the darkness. Use it to drive out the fear, the noises, the excuses. Let it shine brightly, and when given the chance, share the spark with someone you encounter on this journey.

It only takes one spark to bring light into darkness. One spark to drive out fear. One spark to light the flame that becomes a roaring fire. Please, be a spark in that darkness. Spread the light.

Bibliography

Calkins, Lucy McCormick. *The Art of Teaching Writing*. Portsmouth, NH: Heinemann, 1994.

Fletcher, Ralph. *A Writer's Notebook: Unlocking the Writer Within You*. n.p.: HarperTrophy, 1996.

Fox, Mem. "Notes from the Battleground." *Mem Fox* (blog), August 6, 2013, memfox.com/for-teachers/for-teachers-notes-from-the-battlefield.

Heard, Georgia. *Writing Towards Home: Tales and Lessons to Find Your Way*. Portsmouth, NH: Heinemann, 1995.

Kittle, Penny. *Write Beside Them: Risk, Voice, and Clarity in High School Writing*. Portsmouth, NH: Heinemann, 2008.

Lesesne, Teri. *Reading Ladders: Leading Students from Where They Are to Where We'd Like Them to Be*. Portsmouth, NH: Heinemann, 2010.

Murray, Don. *The Essential Don Murray: Lessons from America's Greatest Writing Teacher*, Edited by Thomas Newkirk and Lisa C. Miller. Portsmouth, NH: Heinemann, 2009.

Rief, Linda. *Seeking Diversity: Language Arts with Adolescents*. Portsmouth, NH: Heinemann, 1995.

Winfrey, Oprah. *The Powerful Lesson Maya Angelou Taught Oprah*. Oprah.com video, 4:15. October 19, 2011. oprah.com/oprahs-lifeclass/the-powerful-lesson-maya-angelou-taught-oprah-video.

Acknowledgments

Travis:

The creation of the book you hold in your hands is the result of deep thinking, voracious reading, and a commitment to bringing ideas, stories, and strategies together into one text. There are writers whose voices resonated in my mind as I wrote drafts in my notebook, whose understanding of the craft of teaching propelled my thinking and helped me find a voice of my own. To those writers, teachers, and thinkers, I am eternally grateful.

To my parents, sister, and brother, the people who first knew me as a writer, I extend my utmost appreciation. You encouraged my curiosity, listened as I told stories, read the poems, songs, and stories I wrote, and gave me feedback about the pieces of writing I thought were meaningful. You were my first critics. Thank you for allowing me opportunities to chase my passions.

To Dave and Shelley Burgess, my first publishers, I offer my humblest gratitude. You gave me the chance to share my voice, weaving my experience and ideas into a book that I am so very proud of. Thank you for allowing me to dwell in this possibility. I have loved working with you both.

To Martha Page, the educator and friend who believed in me and invited me to NCTE for the first time, I offer my sincerest gratitude. You showed me the way and continue to guide me in my work with readers and writers. I look to you for methods and ideas that will challenge my thinking. Your beautiful way of teaching has breathed life into lessons, and ultimately, my students are the beneficiaries of your wisdom. You are a rock I lean on. Thank you for the passion you continue to reignite in my teaching life.

To Lisa Harrington, my principal, I offer my appreciation for the support you provide each year. You gave me the latitude to try a writing and reading workshop in my classroom and listened as I philosophized about methodology, strategy, and ways to engage students in content-area classrooms. You have challenged me to think outside of the proverbial box and to share my ideas with colleagues, both local and nationwide. Thank you for working alongside me.

To Cristi Julsrud, my dear friend and fellow teacher, you have stood beside me for years. It all started with *A Midsummer Night's Dream* and has blossomed into our beautiful friendship. You are the colleague whose meaningful understanding of language arts helped lead us into the work we do today with adolescents. I'll never forget the day you came into my classroom, fell to the floor (downstage!), and proclaimed that there must be a better way to reach students. We wanted students to leave our classes with a love for reading and writing, and because of our work together, we are closer to reaching every child we teach. Thank you for being a writing group partner, a book club member (can we even call it that?), and a fellow aficionado of all things literate and delightful. You are a definitely a spark in the dark.

To Mary Howard and Laura Robb, mentors and friends—I don't even know where to begin. You both nudged me further in my teaching this year and only asked that I trust the process. I'll never forget your words, your kindness, and your sheer brilliance.

To my students, past and present, the ones who challenged me and helped me grow into the educator I am today, I am sending the biggest hug and all the love I can muster. I am a better teacher because of you.

And finally, to Todd, my friend, confidant, and co-writer, I owe so much to you. You read my work, shared it on social media, reached out to me, and gave me the chance of a lifetime. I love your willingness to listen to me rave about books, talk through tough teaching moments, and help me seek a deeper understanding in my role as a teacher and human being. I also love that you accepted that I will never write in the shared document until I have explored an idea in my writing notebook, even if it's the night before the manuscript is due. Just so you know, that will never change (hope you're smiling). We make a wonderful team, and I look forward to more projects in the future. Whether it's an article, a blog post, or another book, I can't wait to stand beside your thinking again. Thank you . . . a thousand times over.

Todd:

The acknowledgments section of a book is always the most difficult part for me to write. There are so many people who play a daily role into the man and educator I am today.

I have to start of course with my mom, to whom this book is dedicated. My mom taught reading and writing for thirteen years before unexpectedly passing while I was finishing this book. She was so excited to read this book as she felt like it was a book I was writing for her. Little did I know that I'd be writing about the woman I once knew, who now is no longer with us. Without my mom, this book wouldn't have happened. She was my cheerleader, my rock, my encourager, my friend, my supporter, my challenger, and so much more. She helped me believe that I could do anything, and she loved me when I felt my most unlovable. This book is truly for you, Mom.

To Dave and Shelley Burgess. This is book three guys! WOW! I can't even believe it. I never thought I would write one book, much less three. I am so thankful to have found two people who support me, encourage me, and allow me to be me. You two have been friends and mentors, and I am so thankful to have you behind me and supporting my work. You've truly changed my life.

To Premiere Speakers and especially Ryan Giffen. You guys have given me so many opportunities to share my passion with others from around the world, and I couldn't be more thankful. But Ryan, growing a friendship with you has been the best part. You make me think about things differently, you pray over me, and you are always there as a listening ear when I need advice. I admire you as a colleague, friend, and father. Thank you for always leading by example.

To my 2%. My brothers. No words are enough.

To my mentors and friends near and far. Those who have pushed me, questioned me, challenged my thinking, and never given up on me. I could list you all here, but inevitably I would leave someone off. You know who you are. From the late night (or early morning) phone calls and texts. To the rambling voxer messages or super long emails. To the conversations spoken only in GIFs. I couldn't have made it through the writing of this book (or the last year) without you. From the bottom of my heart, with every ounce of my being, thank you.

To Liz, my wife. We have been through so much and you have allowed me to pursue my dreams and passions. You have the biggest heart and have put up with so much craziness from me. Even in the midst of all the crazy, our quiet moments are my favorite.

To you, the reader. Every time you pick up one of my books and put the faith in my words, I am in awe. I never thought I would write something others would want to read. You have stuck with me (many of you through all three books, so far!). I thank you for the kind words and the questioning of some of my ideas! You make me want to be better for all kids and all educators.

And finally, to Travis. Where do I even start with you? This whole friendship stemmed from me being enlightened by your work and begging you to write a blog post with me. Who knew that we'd become the best of friends, brothers, and of course, TNT. We make such a dynamite team and you truly are a friend for life. You've helped me find my voice and given me such a deep passion for consuming literature I'd thought I'd never have an interest in. You challenge my thinking and never allow me to rest on what I've always believed. You encourage me, are patient beyond belief, and you never cease to amaze me with your compassion for others. I hope to one day be half the man and writer you are. Thank you for taking this journey with me. And as we always say to each other . . . this is only the beginning!

More From

![Dave Burgess Consulting, Inc.]

DAVE BURGESS
Consulting, Inc.

Teach Like a PIRATE

Increase Student Engagement, Boost Your Creativity, and Transform Your Life as an Educator

By Dave Burgess (@BurgessDave)

New York Times' bestseller *Teach Like a PIRATE* sparked a worldwide educational revolution with its passionate teaching manifesto and dynamic student-engagement strategies. Translated into multiple languages, it sparks outrageously creative lessons and life-changing student experiences.

Kids Deserve It!

Pushing Boundaries and Challenging Conventional Thinking

By Todd Nesloney and Adam Welcome (@TechNinjaTodd, @awelcome)

Think big. Make learning fun and meaningful. *Kids Deserve It!* Nesloney and Welcome offer high-tech, high-touch, and highly engaging practices that inspire risk-taking and shake up the status quo on behalf of your students. Rediscover why you became an educator, too!

Stories from Webb

The Ideas, Passions, and Convictions of a Principal and His School Family

By Todd Nesloney (@TechNinjaTodd)

Stories from Webb goes right to the heart of education. Told by award-winning principal Todd Nesloney and his dedicated team of staff and teachers, this book reminds you why you became an educator. Relatable stories reinvigorate and may inspire you to tell your own!

Learn Like a PIRATE

Empower Your Students to Collaborate, Lead, and Succeed

By Paul Solarz (@PaulSolarz)

Passing grades don't equip students for life and career responsibilities. *Learn Like a PIRATE* shows how risk-taking and exploring passions in stimulating, motivating, supportive, self-directed classrooms creates students capable of making smart, responsible decisions on their own.

P is for PIRATE

Inspirational ABC's for Educators

By Dave and Shelley Burgess (@Burgess_Shelley)

In *P is for Pirate*, husband-and-wife team Dave and Shelley Burgess tap personal experiences of seventy educators to inspire others to create fun and exciting places to learn. It's a wealth of imaginative and creative ideas that makes learning and teaching more fulfilling than ever before.

Play Like a Pirate

Engage Students with Toys, Games, and Comics

By Quinn Rollins (@jedikermit)

In *Play Like a Pirate*, Quinn Rollins offers practical, engaging strategies and resources that make it easy to integrate fun into your curriculum. Regardless of grade level, serious learning can be seriously fun with inspirational ideas that engage students in unforgettable ways.

eXPlore Like a Pirate

Gamification and Game-Inspired Course Design to Engage, Enrich, and Elevate Your Learners

By Michael Matera (@MrMatera)

Create an experiential, collaborative, and creative world with classroom game designer and educator Michael Matera's game-based learning book, *eXPlore Like a Pirate*. Matera helps teachers apply motivational gameplay techniques and enhance curriculum with gamification strategies.

Pure Genius

Building a Culture of Innovation and Taking 20% Time to the Next Level

By Don Wettrick (@DonWettrick)

Collaboration—with experts, students, and other educators—helps create interesting and even life-changing opportunities for learning. In *Pure Genius*, Don Wettrick inspires and equips educators with a systematic blueprint for beating classroom boredom and teaching innovation.

The Zen Teacher

Creating Focus, Simplicity, and Tranquility in the Classroom

By Dan Tricarico (@thezenteacher)

Unrushed and fully focused, teachers influence—even improve—the future when they maximize performance and improve their quality of life. In *The Zen Teacher*, Dan Tricarico offers practical, easy-to-use techniques to develop a non-religious Zen practice and thrive in the classroom.

140 Twitter Tips for Educators

Get Connected, Grow Your Professional Learning Network, and Reinvigorate Your Career

By Brad Currie, Billy Krakower, and Scott Rocco (@bradmcurrie, @wkrakower, @ScottRRocco)

In *140 Twitter Tips for Educators*, #Satchat hosts and founders of Evolving Educators, Brad Currie, Billy Krakower, and Scott Rocco, offer step-by-step instruction on Twitter basics and building an online following within Twitter's vibrant network of educational professionals.

The Innovator's Mindset

Empower Learning, Unleash Talent, and Lead a Culture of Creativity

By George Couros (@gcouros)

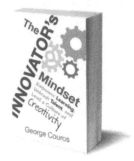

In *The Innovator's Mindset*, teachers and administrators discover that compliance to a scheduled curriculum hinders student innovation, critical thinking, and creativity. To become forward-thinking leaders, students must be empowered to wonder and explore.

50 Things You Can Do with Google Classroom

By Alice Keeler and Libbi Miller
(@alicekeeler, @MillerLibbi)

50 Things You Can Do with Google Classroom provides a thorough overview of this GAfE app and shortens the teacher learning curve for introducing technology in the classroom. Keeler and Miller's ideas, instruction, and screenshots help teachers go digital with this powerful tool.

50 Things to Go Further with Google Classroom

A Student-Centered Approach

By Alice Keeler and Libbi Miller
(@alicekeeler, @MillerLibbi)

In *50 Things to Go Further with Google Classroom: A Student-Centered Approach*, authors and educators Alice Keeler and Libbi Miller help teachers create a digitally rich, engaging, student-centered environment that taps the power of individualized learning using Google Classroom.

The Writing on the Classroom Wall

How Posting Your Most Passionate Beliefs about Education Can Empower Your Students, Propel Your Growth, and Lead to a Lifetime of Learning

By Steve Wyborney (@SteveWyborney)

Big ideas lead to deeper learning, but they don't have to be profound to have profound impact. Teacher Steve Wyborney explains why and how sharing ideas sharpens and refines them. It's okay if some ideas fall off the wall; what matters most is sharing and discussing.

Master the Media

*How Teaching Media Literacy Can
Save Our Plugged-in World*

By Julie Smith (@julnilsmith)

Master the Media explains media history, purpose, and messaging so teachers and parents can empower students with critical-thinking skills which lead to informed choices, the ability to differentiate between truth and lies, and discern perception from reality. Media literacy can save the world.

The Classroom Chef

*Sharpen your lessons. Season your classes.
Make math meaningful.*

By John Stevens and Matt Vaudrey
(@Jstevens009, @MrVaudrey)

With imagination and preparation, every teacher can be *The Classroom Chef* using John Stevens and Matt Vaudrey's secret recipes, ingredients, and tips that help students "get" math. Use ideas as-is, or tweak to create enticing educational meals that engage students.

Ditch That Textbook

*Free Your Teaching and Revolutionize
Your Classroom*

By Matt Miller (@jmattmiller)

Ditch That Textbook creates a support system, toolbox, and manifesto that can free teachers from outdated textbooks. Miller empowers them to untether themselves, throw out meaningless, pedestrian teaching and learning practices, and evolve and revolutionize their classrooms.

Your School Rocks ... So Tell People!

*Passionately Pitch and Promote the Positives
Happening on Your Campus*

By Ryan McLane and Eric Lowe
(@McLane_Ryan, @EricLowe21)

Your School Rocks . . . So Tell People! helps schools create effective social media communication strategies that keep students' families and the community connected to what's going on at school, offering more than seventy immediately actionable tips with easy-to-follow instructions and video tutorial links.

How Much Water Do We Have?

5 Success Principles for Conquering Any Change and Thriving in Times of Change

By Pete Nunweiler with Kris Nunweiler

Stressed out, overwhelmed, or uncertain at work or home? It could be figurative dehydration. *How Much Water Do We Have?* identifies five key elements necessary for success of any goal, life transition, or challenge. Learn to find, acquire, and use the 5 Waters of Success.

Instant Relevance

Using Today's Experiences in Tomorrow's Lessons

By Denis Sheeran (@MathDenisNJ)

Learning sticks when it's relevant to students. In *Instant Relevance*, author and keynote speaker Denis Sheeran equips you to create engaging lessons from experiences and events that matter to students while helping them make meaningful connections between the real world and the classroom.

Launch

Using Design Thinking to Boost Creativity and Bring Out the Maker in Every Student

By John Spencer and A.J. Juliani
(@spencerideas, @ajjuliani)

When students identify themselves as makers, inventors, and creators, they discover powerful problem-solving and critical-thinking skills. Their imaginations and creativity will shape our future. John Spencer and A.J. Juliani's *LAUNCH* process dares you to innovate and empower them.

Teaching Math with Google Apps

50 G Suite Activities, Vol. 1

By Alice Keeler and Diana Herrington
(@alicekeeler, @mathdiana)

Teaching Math with Google Apps meshes the easy student/teacher interaction of Google Apps with G Suite that empowers student creativity and critical thinking. Keeler and Herrington demonstrate fifty ways to bring math classes into the twenty-first century with easy-to-use technology.

Escaping the School Leader's Dunk Tank

How to Prevail When Others Want to See You Drown

By Rebecca Coda and Rick Jetter
(@RebeccaCoda, @RickJetter)

Dunk-tank situations—discrimination, bad politics, revenge, or ego-driven coworkers—can make an educator's life miserable. Coda and Jetter (dunk-tank survivors themselves) share real-life stories and insightful research to equip school leaders with tools to survive and, better yet, avoid getting "dunked."

Start. Right. Now.

Teach and Lead for Excellence

By Todd Whitaker, Jeff Zoul, and Jimmy Casas
(@ToddWhitaker, @Jeff_Zoul, @casas_jimmy)

Excellent leaders and teachers *Know the Way, Show the Way, Go the Way, and Grow Each Day.* Whitaker, Zoul, and Casas share four key behaviors of excellence from educators across the U.S. and motivate to put you on the right path.

Lead Like a PIRATE

Make School Amazing for Your Students and Staff

By Shelley Burgess and Beth Houf
(@Burgess_Shelley, @BethHouf)

Lead Like a PIRATE maps out character traits necessary to captain a school or district. You'll learn where to find treasure already in your classrooms and schools—and bring out the best in educators. Find encouragement in your relentless quest to make school amazing for everyone!

Table Talk Math

A Practical Guide for Bringing Math into Everyday Conversations

By John Stevens (@Jstevens009)

In *Table Talk Math*, John Stevens offers parents—and teachers—ideas for initiating authentic, math-based, everyday conversations that get kids to notice and pique their curiosity about the numbers, patterns, and equations in the world around them.

Shift This!

How to Implement Gradual Change for Massive Impact in Your Classroom

By Joy Kirr (@JoyKirr)

Establishing a student-led culture focused on individual responsibility and personalized learning is possible, sustainable, and even easy when it happens little by little. In *Shift This!*, Joy Kirr details gradual shifts in thinking, teaching, and approach for massive impact in your classroom.

Unmapped Potential

An Educator's Guide to Lasting Change

By Julie Hasson and Missy Lennard (@PPrincipals)

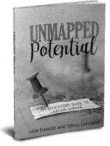

Overwhelmed and overworked? You're not alone, but it can get better. You simply need the right map to guide you from frustrated to fulfilled. *Unmapped Potential* offers advice and practical strategies to forge a unique path to becoming the educator and person you want to be.

Shattering the Perfect Teacher Myth

6 Truths That Will Help You THRIVE as an Educator

By Aaron Hogan (@aaron_hogan)

Author and educator Aaron Hogan helps shatter the idyllic "perfect teacher" myth, which erodes self-confidence with unrealistic expectations and sets teachers up for failure. His book equips educators with strategies that help them shift out of survival mode and THRIVE.

Social LEADia

Moving Students from Digital Citizenship to Digital Leadership

By Jennifer Casa-Todd (@JCasaTodd)

A networked society requires students to leverage social media to connect to people, passions, and opportunities to grow and make a difference. *Social LEADia* helps shift focus at school and home from digital citizenship to digital leadership and equip students for the future.

Spark Learning

3 Keys to Embracing the Power of Student Curiosity

By Ramsey Musallam (@ramusallam)

Inspired by his popular TED Talk "3 Rules to Spark Learning," Musallam combines brain science research, proven teaching methods, and his personal story to empower you to improve your students' learning experiences by inspiring inquiry and harnessing its benefits.

Ditch That Homework

Practical Strategies to Help Make Homework Obsolete

By Matt Miller and Alice Keeler (@jmattmiller, @alicekeeler)

In *Ditch That Homework*, Miller and Keeler discuss the pros and cons of homework, why it's assigned, and what life could look like without it. They evaluate research, share parent and teacher insights, then make a convincing case for ditching it for effective and personalized learning methods.

The Four O'Clock Faculty

A Rogue Guide to Revolutionizing Professional Development

By Rich Czyz (@RACzyz)

In *The Four O'Clock Faculty*, Rich identifies ways to make professional learning meaningful, efficient, and, above all, personally relevant. It's a practical guide to revolutionize PD, revealing why some is so awful and what you can do to change the model for the betterment of everyone.

Culturize

Every Student. Every Day. Whatever It Takes.

By Jimmy Casas (@casas_jimmy)

Culturize dives into what it takes to cultivate a community of learners who embody innately human traits our world desperately needs—kindness, honesty, and compassion. Casas's stories reveal how "soft skills" can be honed while exceeding academic standards of twenty-first-century learning.

Code Breaker

Increase Creativity, Remix Assessment, and Develop a Class of Coder Ninjas!

By Brian Aspinall (@mraspinall)

You don't have to be a "computer geek" to use coding to turn curriculum expectations into student skills. Use *Code Breaker* to teach students how to identify problems, develop solutions, and use computational thinking to apply and demonstrate learning.

The Wild Card

7 Steps to an Educator's Creative Breakthrough

By Hope and Wade King (@hopekingteach, @wadeking7)

The Kings facilitate a creative breakthrough in the classroom with *The Wild Card*, a step-by-step guide to drawing on your authentic self to deliver your content creatively and be the wild card who changes the game for your learners.

The Principled Principal

10 Principles for Leading Exceptional Schools

By Jeffrey Zoul and Anthony McConnell (@Jeff_Zoul, @mcconnellaw)

Zoul and McConnell know from personal experience that the role of school principal is one of the most challenging and the most rewarding in education. Using relatable stories and real-life examples, they reveal ten core values that will empower you to work and lead with excellence.

The Limitless School

Creative Ways to Solve the Culture Puzzle

By Abe Hege and Adam Dovico (@abehege, @adamdovico)

Being intentional about creating a positive culture is imperative for your school's success. This book identifies the nine pillars that support a positive school culture and explains how each stakeholder has a vital role to play in the work of making schools safe, inviting, and dynamic.

Google Apps for Littles

Believe They Can

By Christine Pinto and Alice Keeler
(@PintoBeanz11, @alicekeeler)

Learn how to tap into students' natural curiosity using technology. Pinto and Keeler share a wealth of innovative ways to integrate digital tools in the primary classroom to make learning engaging and relevant for even the youngest of today's twenty-first-century learners.

Be the One for Kids

You Have the Power to Change the Life of a Child

By Ryan Sheehy (@sheehyrw)

Students need guidance to succeed academically, but they also need our help to survive and thrive in today's turbulent world. They need someone to model the attributes that will help them win not just in school but in life as well. That someone is you.

Let Them Speak

How Student Voice Can Transform Your School

By Rebecca Coda and Rick Jetter (@RebeccaCoda, @RickJetter)

We say, "Student voice matters," but are we really listening? This book will inspire you to find out what your students really think, feel, and need. You'll learn how to listen to and use student feedback to improve your school's culture. All you have to do is ask—and then *Let Them Speak*.

The EduProtocol Field Guide

16 Student-Centered Lesson Frames for Infinite Learning Possibilities

By Marlena Hebren and Jon Corippo (@mhebern, @jcorippo)

Are you ready to break out of the lesson-and-worksheet rut? Use *The EduProtocol Field Guide* to create engaging and effective instruction, build culture, and deliver content to K–12 students in a supportive, creative environment.

All 4s and 5s

A Guide to Teaching and Leading Advanced
Placement Programs

By Andrew Sharos (@AndrewSharosAP)

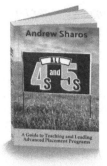

AP classes shouldn't be relegated to "privileged" schools and students. With proper support, every student can experience success. *All 4s and 5s* offers a wealth of classroom and program strategies that equip you to develop a culture of academic and personal excellence.

Shake Up Learning

Practical Ideas to Move Learning from
Static to Dynamic

By Kasey Bell (@ShakeUpLearning)

Is the learning in your classroom static or dynamic? *Shake Up Learning* guides you through the process of creating dynamic learning opportunities—from purposeful planning and maximizing technology to fearless implementation.

The Secret Solution

How One Principal Discovered the Path to Success

By Todd Whitaker, Sam Miller, and Ryan Donlan (@ToddWhitaker, @SamMiller29, @RyanDonlan)

This entertaining parable provides leaders with a non-threatening tool to discuss problematic attitudes in schools. In the updated edition, you'll find a reader's guide to help you identify habits and traits that can propel you and your team to success.

The Path to Serendipity

Discover the Gifts along Life's Journey

By Allyson Apsey (@AllysonApsey)

In this funny, genuine, and clever book, Allyson Apsey shares relatable stories and practical strategies for living a meaningful life regardless of the craziness happening around you. You'll discover that you really do have the power to choose the kind of life you live—every day.

Lead with Culture

What Really Matters in Our Schools

By Jay Billy (@JayBilly2)

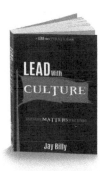

In this *Lead Like a PIRATE Guide*, Jay Billy explains that making school a place where students and staff want to be starts with culture. You'll be inspired by this principal's practical ideas for creating a sense of unity—even in the most diverse communities.

The Pepper Effect

Tap into the Magic of Creativity, Collaboration, and Innovation

By Sean Gaillard (@smgaillard)

Using *Sgt. Pepper's Lonely Hearts Club Band* by The Beatles as a template for inspiration, Sean Gaillard explores the necessary steps for creating the conditions for motivation, collaboration, creativity, and innovation in *your* schoolhouse.

The EduNinja Mindset

11 Habits for Building a Stronger Mind and Body

By Jennifer Burdis (@jennifer_burdis)

As a two-time *American Ninja Warrior* contestant, educator, and trainer, Jen Burdis pushes herself to physically and mentally overcome obstacles. In *The EduNinja Mindset*, Burdis shares her strategies to empower teachers, students and families to develop healthy habits.

About the Authors

TRAVIS CROWDER is a passionate educator, reader, and writer. He is a National Board Certified teacher who currently teaches seventh-grade English/language arts and social studies in North Carolina. His teaching career has also included teaching eighth-grade English/language arts and work in high school with ninth- and twelfth-grade students.

Travis is committed to the belief that everyone can fall in love with reading and writing. If they claim otherwise, they just haven't found the right book or topic that will engage their heart and mind. Travis loves connecting students (and adults) with books based on their interests and is well known for his passionate book talks. Travis has written for the Nerdy Book Club, Scholastic Reader Leader, National Association of Elementary School Principals, International Literacy Association, and many more.

Travis shares his love of literacy and learning at trainings and conferences nationwide. He is also the co-host of the podcast series "Sparks in the Dark."

You can learn more about Travis at his website: teachermantrav.com. Connect with him on Twitter: @TeacherManTrav.

TODD NESLONEY is an educator down to his core. Whether it's working with kids or adults, Todd loves sharing his passion of learning. He currently serves as a principal and lead learner in Texas. Prior to working in this capacity, Todd taught in the fourth and fifth grades for seven years.

Todd was recognized by President Barack Obama as a White House Champion of Change and by the National School Board Association as a "20 to Watch" in Education. He was recognized by the Texas Computer Education Association (TCEA) as their Elementary Teacher of the Year and selected by the Center for Digital Education as one of the "Top 40 Innovators in Education." He was the 2015 BAMMY Award recipient for Elementary Principal of the Year and the 2014 BAMMY Award recipient for Classroom Teacher of the Year.

Todd is the author of *Stories from Webb*, children's book *Spruce & Lucy*, and coauthor of the award-winning book *Flipping 2.0: Practical Strategies for Flipping Your Classroom*, as well as the coauthor of *Kids Deserve It!* Todd also co-hosts a top-rated iTunes show, "Kids Deserve It!" and "Sparks in the Dark." Todd shares his journey online through videos on his professional Facebook page as well.

Todd is passionate about eliminating excuses, innovative practices, and doing what's best for kids. In addition to his career as an administrator and educator, Todd leads staff developments and gives keynotes at districts and conferences around the world.

You can learn more about Todd at his website toddnesloney.com. Connect with him on Twitter: @TechNinjaTodd.